The Methuen
Classical

Chrys Salt is a
She is Artistic D
Theatre Compa
sound and has worked with many of the country's leading
actors. She has written several books including her popular
book for actors, *Make Acting Work*, and edited six collections
of monologues. In addition, she has written theatre and
radio plays, documentaries and poetry. She is a regular tutor
at the London Actors Centre.

The Methuen Book of Classical Monologues for Women

Edited by
CHRYS SALT

Methuen Drama

First published by Methuen 2005

Methuen Publishing Limited
11–12 Buckingham Gate
London SW1E 6LB

10 9 8 7 6 5 4 3 2 1

Copyright in this selection © Chrys Salt, 2005

Methuen Publishing Ltd Reg. No. 3543167

A CIP catalogue record for this book is available from the British Library

ISBN 0 413 77534 8

Typeset by SX Composing DTP, Rayleigh, Essex
Printed and bound in Great Britain by
Bookmarque Ltd, Croydon, Surrey

Disclaimer
Methuen Publishing Limited gratefully acknowledges the permissions granted
to reproduce the quoted extracts within this work. Every effort has been made to
trace the current copyright holders of the extracts included in this work. The
publishers apologise for any unintended omissions and would be pleased to
receive any information that would enable them to amend any inaccuracies or
omissions in future editions.

Contents

Introduction by Chrys Salt   1

Classical Greek

Atossa from *Persians* by Aeschylus   8
Medea from *Medea* by Euripides/Liz Lochhead   10
Alcestis from *Alcestis* by Euripides   14
Iphigeneia from *Iph. . . (Iphigenia in Aulis)* by
   Euripides/Colin Teevan   18

Elizabethan and Jacobean English

Zenocrate from *Tamburlaine the Great* by Christopher Marlowe   22
Alice Arden from *Arden of Feversham* (anon)   24
Titania from *A Midsummer Night's Dream*
   by William Shakespeare   26
Portia from *Julius Caesar* by William Shakespeare   30
Celia from *Volpone* by Ben Jonson   34
Mistress Mulligrub from *The Dutch Courtesan*
   by John Marston   36
Duchess from *The Revenger's Tragedy*
   attributed to Cyril Tourner   38
Bianca from *Women Beware Women*
   by Thomas Middleton   40
Queen Katharine from *Henry VIII*
   by William Shakespeare   42
Beatrice-Joanna from *The Changeling*
   by Thomas Middleton and William Rowley   44
Penthea from *The Broken Heart* by John Ford   48
Putana from *'Tis Pity She's a Whore* by John Ford   50

Restoration and Eighteenth-Century British

Lady Plyant from *The Double Dealer* by William Congreve   52
Angelica from *Love for Love* by William Congreve   54

Berinthia from *The Relapse* by Sir John Vanburgh 56
Lady Wishfort from *The Way of the World*
  by William Congreve 58
Mrs Sullen from *The Beaux' Stratagem* by George Farquhar 60
Julia from *the Rivals* by Richard Brinsley Sheridan 62
Helen from *The Family Legend* by Joanna Baillie 64

French, Spanish and Italian

Mencía from *The Surgeon of Honour* by Calderón de la Barca 66
Agnès from *The School for Wives* by Molière 68
Elmire from *Tartuffe* by Molière 72
Frostine from *The Miser* by Molière 76
Albina from *Britannicus* by Jean Racine 80
Lisette from *Careless Vows* by Pierre Marivaux 82
Mirandolina from *Mirandolina* by Carlo Goldoni 84
Marceline from *The Marriage of Figaro* by Beaumarchais 86
Lucretia from *Lucretia Borgia* by Victor Hugo 90
Mathilde from *Caprice* by Alfred de Musset 94

Russian and Scandinavian

Agafya from *Marriage* by Nikolai Gogol 96
Darya Ivanovna from *A Provincial Lady* by Ivan Turgenev 98
Katerina from *The Thunderstorm* by Alexander Ostrovsky 102
Natalia from *A Month in the Country* by Ivan Turgenev 104
Mrs Alving from *Ghosts* by Henrik Ibsen 106
Yelena from *Uncle Vanya* by Anton Chekhov 110
Irena Serghyeevna from *Three Sisters* by Anton Chekhov 112

Acknowledgements 114

Introduction

When you are called to audition, you will either be asked to do a 'cold' reading or perform something from your audition repertoire. You'll certainly need a handful of pieces under your belt whether it's the usual 'one classical and one contemporary piece' for drama school entry or a piece for a specific audition.

Your job at audition is not only to show that you might be right for *this particular job*, but that you are an artist with talent and imagination – so even if you are not 'right' this time round you will stick in my mind when she/he's casting again.

This is a selection of classical texts ranging from Aeschylus to Chekhov. Even if you don't have an audition coming up it's valuable experience to research a play and learn a speech. (One young actor I know was asked for nine audition pieces over the course of three recalls for a repertory season, so you can never have too many pieces.) Practise them regularly so you are not caught on the hop when the phone rings. It keeps your mind alive and your creative juices flowing.

So how does acting in the classics differ from acting in modern plays, and how do you choose a part that's right for you?

When you are choosing your classical repertoire, think carefully about how many pieces you need and what you are auditioning for. No good wheeling out your Jacobean revenge tragedy for an audition for *The Relapse* or helpful to render your lyrical heroine if you are fully forty-two and look like an escapee from *EastEnders*. Even when auditioning for the classics you still need to find something appropriate – a role for which you might actually be considered. I know, I know, you became an actor to demonstrate your versatility and transform from within. Nevertheless, you are still limited by age, experience, education, class, vocal range and physical appearance, so be realistic. After all, these are the unique raw materials of your art. Nobody else is like you.

When I was writing my book *Make Acting Work*, I had an interesting chat with Jude Kelly (former Artistic Director of the West

Yorkshire Playhouse) about 'typecasting'– unpopular as it is. I'll quote it again because you might bear it in mind when deciding which pieces to choose.

> It's very hard to make actors understand that you are often not turning them down because they are less good than somebody else – you turn them down because they are not . . . right in some way. Actors get very upset about this and yet if you ask them what they think of such and such a production, they often say 'So and so was completely wrong for that part.' At the same time they will be arguing for a completely level playing field without any version of 'typecasting' at all . . .

Classical texts present different challenges to actors than modern ones, making greater demands on stamina, imagination, vocal flexibility and breath control. Make sure you keep fit and do your breathing exercises every day so you are in good shape – something every actor should be doing anyway. The characters use language that is alien, syntax with which we are not familiar and words that are not in our vocabulary. Sometimes texts are written in verse; language is heightened and carries complex, lengthy thought processes, imposing another range of problems. If the text is written in verse do you sacrifice its structure, rhymes and rhythms to a more colloquial tone? How do you sustain the measure and cadence of the poetry but at the same time expose the layers of emotion and meaning it carries? How can you make these texts communicate to modern audiences? How do we make these seemingly 'larger then life' characters live and breathe when their situations and modes of expression seem so unfamiliar? Just how much breath do you *need* to carry sense across five lines of iambic pentameter? No wonder actors approach classical text with trepidation.

You won't expect me to write an essay on classical acting in an audition book, but I can give you a few tips that might help with these speeches. A couple of minutes is a short space of time for you to 'strut your stuff' so I hope my comments will help maximize your opportunities. I have tried to give you as much information as I can in the body of the text about context, and supply meanings for words and expressions not in common usage. I hope the following will be an adjunct to these.

- Read the play. You can't hope to glean all you need to know about a character and his situation from a single speech, or indeed from my commentaries.
- Learn the text accurately (you can't paraphrase Congreve or improvise iambic pentameter) and find out every last thing you can about your character and her journey through the play. Where are you? Where have you come from? Where are you headed? What do other characters have to say about you? Where does the character hail from and what accent might she use? Research the period, the social mores and the costume. What you character is wearing will make a difference to our posture and demeanour – you can't bend in the middle in a corset. What do you want? Money? Power? Love? What drives you? Lust? Hatred? Ambition? Revenge? Why are you saying this now? What is your relationship with the person you are talking to? Lover? Enemy? Rival? Or, indeed, with the audience? Maybe you are alone onstage, talking to yourself, admitting the audience right inside your head, making them privy to your innermost thoughts and conflicts, or making a direct address, treating them like friends, co-conspirators or confidantes? Sharing your glee? Seeking their approval? Perhaps you are stepping out of the action to make an observation to them that other characters can't hear? What is the style of the play? Where is it set? Is it a comedy or tragedy? All this needs careful thought.
- Play the situation. Play the intention. Play the relationship. If you find the text difficult, translate it into colloquial English. Speak it aloud then return to the original with your 'translation' in mind. Rehearse until it sits easily on your tongue. Make sure you understand it. Unpick it and struggle with it until you do. You can't make an audience understand what you don't completely understand yourself. Nor can you make any emotional

connection with it. If the text is obscure, the subtext must be crystal. What do you actually mean by what you say? Characters interact and express themselves via means other than text.

- If the text is written in verse tune your ear to its rhythms, rhymes and resonance; observe the punctuation, the length of lines and line endings – these often give clues to emphasis, changes of gear, the pace at which a character speaks, thought transitions or watchful silences. Note repetitions or where a regular rhythm changes and ask yourself why this might be. For instance, take these lines from Alcestis' farewell speech to her husband in Euripides by *Alcestis*. What can we learn from unpicking them?

> Seeing I must die . . . 'Tis here, across my way,
> Not for tomorrow, not for the third day,
> But now – Death, and to lie with things that were.
> Farewell.

Read it aloud – strictly observing the rhythm. It is iambic pentameter, but line two doesn't quite scan, does it? Read it again carefully observing the punctuation. What does the word 'must' tell us? She has no options. Not 'might' or 'will' but 'must'. Why the ellipsis? A pause to consider the weight of what she has just said – what death actually means? Give time for the realisation to sink in. Here! Just across the road! Not the next day, or the next. The immediacy of it! Then iambic pentameter dislocates as the reality sinks in. Although the first two lines are a rhyming couplet, the sense of the sentence arcs across into line three. The dash after 'now'. And 'now' juxtaposed with Death. The finality! Why the capital letter for Death? It is not the beginning of a sentence. Death has a persona – like a lover she must lie with as she did with her Husband (also capitalised throughout the text to give him due importance). Death is the subject of the sentence. It demands special emphasis. The length of the sentence suggests painful, yet thoughtful consideration. Her death is close and she is struggling for breath. Try reading it in a panic or in tears. Doesn't work, does it? Look how the translator has inset 'Farewell' – a short space as

Alcestis moves on from her acceptance of the inevitable to her heartbreaking 'goodbyes'.

Thus an enormous amount of information can be wrested from even a very small amount of text with minimum knowledge of its context. It is careful work that will reward your efforts.

Not too many of us experience being seduced by our own brother like Annabella in *'Tis Pity She's a Whore*, but we can understand the sexual passion that drives them. It doesn't take a leap of imagination to put yourself in her shoes. The characters might be larger than life, their emotions heightened, the language from another age, but these plays were written to be spoken by actors just like you to convey passions no different from our own. They haven't lasted down the centuries without having something pretty powerful to say to audiences today.

My commentaries should not be seen as 'giving direction' in anything but the loosest sense. It is up to you to do your own research and bring your own interpretation to these wonderful roles. There is no 'right way' to play them, and a director will always prick up his ears if you are able to offer an original 'take' on a well-known piece. I have tried to give a few tips and indicators about background, context, interpretation and approach – to point you towards a few clues buried in the language, the structure or the syntax. I have left in stage directions where they seem relevant. Sometimes I have included the whole of a long speech so you can see the 'through line' and then cut it yourself, and on the odd occasion I have linked speeches where the thought process can be sustained when the interlocutor is cut out. I hope you will find this an interesting and varied selection. But more importantly, I hope they help to get that job. Good luck.

This book is dedicated to the memory of my friends Linda Gardner, Caroline Bingham and Carl Forgione, who died too soon and enriched my life.

Atossa from *Persians* by Aeschylus (translated by Frederic Raphael and Kenneth McLeish)

Persians is probably the oldest surviving play in Western literature (472 BC). It is a powerful dramatic poem set at the time of the Persian Wars in the court of King Xerxes and his mother Queen Atossa. After fifty years of warfare during which the Persian Empire attempted to conquer Greece, the Persians are finally defeated. Xerxes has been tricked by a 'double agent' into launching an invasion against Athens, but in spite of the Persian army's superior numbers, their ships are trapped in a narrow strait between the island of Salamis and the mainland. Thousands of men are ambushed and slaughtered by a small advance party of Greeks. Almost the entire Persian army is crushed. Only a few of their ships and their men escape. The ragged survivors, including the dishonoured Xerxes, flee in panic.

At home, Xerxes' mother, fearful and desperate with anxiety, waits for news of the battle and her son's fate. Her faithful dignitaries (the Chorus) try to comfort her by saying things she wants to hear, but Atossa has been having terrible nightmares (dreams are one of the ways the gods communicate with humans) and in this speech she describes them – sharing her fears. They are full of evil portents and foreboding. She seems to be unpicking them. Seeking answers. What do the two beautiful women signify? Do they signify Greece breaking free of the Persian yoke and prophesy Xerxes' defeat? In the dream Darius, Xerxes' father, weeps for him. Xerxes rips his clothes in humiliation and dishonour. What can it mean? On waking, full of apprehension, she relates how she took gifts to placate the gods, but witnesses yet another omen – the spectacle of an eagle being savaged by a much smaller hawk on the sacred altar of Phoebus Apollo. Atossa is clearly shaken by these signs and the last three lines seem full of bravado rather than confidence. 'Know this' is spoken as an instruction. In spite of every evil portent, she is reassuring herself that Xerxes will triumph.

Atossa

Dreams haunt me.
Night after night they come,
Since my son drummed up his army,
Marched on Greece. Dream after dream –
And none so clear as in this last night.
Two women came: well-dressed,
One in Persian elegance, one Dorian.
In bearing both belittled us today:
In beauty flawless sisters;
In race identical. Their native lands?
One Greek, one . . . not-Greek.
Suddenly they quarrelled, the pair of them.
My son separated them, calmed them,
Tried to yoke them to his chariot.
One stood quiet, obedient,
Proud in her harness. The other
Bucked, tore free the bridle, plunged
Out of control, and smashed the yoke.
My son stumbled. Darius came,
His father, and wept for him. When Xerxes saw,
He ripped his own clothes to rags.
That was the dream. When morning came,
In running water I washed away the omen,
Ran to the altar, carrying in my hand –
This hand, the hand ordained –
Gifts to the gods to take all ill away.
Instead, an eagle, fluttering in fear,
Settled on Phoebus' holy hearth.
I watched. Mute with fear.
A hawk next. Swooped, perched – the talons! –
Raking, clawing its rival's head. Down, down,
The eagle cowered. Offered itself. No fight.
I saw this terror, saw as I tell you now.
Know this: My son, successful, will dazzle every eye.
But if he fails, he'll not step down:
Long as he lives, this land is his.

Medea from *Medea* by Euripides (adapted by Liz Lochhead)

This tragedy of 431 BC focuses on Medea, a woman whose jealousy and desire for revenge are unbounded when she discovers her husband Jason has traded her in for a younger model.

The story of Jason and the Argonauts is well known. Jason is deprived of his kingdom of Thessaly by his brother, Pelias. In order to regain it, he is required to capture the fabled Golden Fleece from the King of Colchis. He sets sail on the *Argo*, and after many hair-raising adventures captures the fleece with the aid of the foreign princess Medea, who uses sorcery to help him, then leaves her home, betrays her father and murders her brother. The couple marry and return to Greece with their two sons where Medea again uses her powers to have Pelias killed, but still the throne eludes them and they are forced to flee to Corinth. Once there, the ambitious Jason deserts her for Glauke, the Princess of Corinth, in order to consolidate his position. Fearing Medea's revenge, Glauke's father, Creon, tries to banish Medea and the children before the wedding, but Medea tricks him into allowing her to stay one more day. It is a decision that has the direst consequences.

Medea is a forceful, charismatic and persuasive woman with dangerous powers. Jason has been at the heart of her world and the thought of another woman having him is unbearable. At the beginning of the play her nurse reports how her distraught mistress can't stop crying and raging, and won't eat, sleep or talk.

In this scene, Jason has come to see her to offer the olive branch of his support, and tells her she is lucky her punishment is no worse than banishment after her abusive behaviour towards the King. Heaping insult on injury, he ventures things might be better if she managed to keep her temper in check . . . It is like a red rag to a bull. Medea turns on him with all the pent-up venom at her disposal. She rages, she sneers, she insults – pulling no punches as she reminds him of everything she has given up for him. She rakes over the past, the things she has done for him –

10

supported him through thick and thin, borne his children, burned her boats with her family, lost all her friends, has nowhere to go and this is how he repays her! Hell hath no fury . . . Look at the arrangement of the lines. What does this tell you about the pacing of the speech and Medea's state of mind? Transpose the scene into a modern marriage and the sentiments would not be very different.

'There is an anger that goes beyond all remedy, when love turns to hate,' comments the Chorus. Nothing will stop the terrible engine of Medea's revenge which drives her to kill Glauke and Creon and finally her own children to make Jason suffer appropriate agonies for his betrayal.

Medea

I can't keep it zipped!
who   what   could be worse than you?
I'd call you coward   you piece of vomit   man
who is no man at all except you're man enough to come here
amazing   shamelessness never fails to amaze
d'you think it brave?   how dare you
shit on those you say you love and then come visiting?
where in the depths
of your vile maleness do you get the nerve?
thanks for coming though
for I can ease my heart and watch you squirm

first things first   I saved your life
and everybody knows it   each Greek that sailed with you
the whole caboodle who crewed the valiant *Argo*
knows it   without my magic
you could not have yoked the fiery bulls
in the field of death   nor sown the dragons' teeth
except I killed the serpent whose loathsome coils
looped the Golden Fleece
and who was its guardian who never slept
I killed it   I made you Jason!
betrayed my own father   my royal line
ran mad for you   after you   to Iolcus   Pelias' place
more passion then than sense
I killed King Pelias to keep you secure
killed him by tricking his loving daughters
to unwitting patricide
horror and another royal house destroyed

so I did then   now   so!   do you
cheat on me   forsake me   bed a new bride

I gave you progeny
I'd have seen the force of a fresh liaison

12

were I barren but I bore you sons   you swore by Gods
who must be dead so simply you broke all faith with them
my hand that held yours   I should cut it off
my knees that parted to let you easy come between
defile me   I'm fouled by even memory of your foul touch

so Jason you love me and wish me well?   pray tell
friend   sweet husband   where am I to go?
to my father's house perhaps?   oh yes!
the father I betrayed to go with you
to Pelias' daughters?   they'd welcome me with open arms
that glad we did the old man in!
this is the state I'm in   my friends and family are history
they hate me now
I made enemies of everyone I ever loved
for you   hurt those I had no need to hurt
for you   and in return
you make me the happiest woman in Greece
envied by all   'what a husband   lucky woman
    you could
one hundred percent trust him   to betray you!'
and here's his wedding present to himself
rootless penury for his discarded beggar wife and brats
oh Gods   there're proofs to tell
true gold from fool's dross
why no hallmarks stamped on the hearts of men?

Alcestis from *Alcestis* by Euripides (translated by Gilbert Murray)

Alcestis was first performed in 438 BC. It takes place in and around the ancient castle of Admetus, King of Pherae, in Thessaly.

The play opens with the god Apollo telling the audience how he has negotiated with the underworld to spare Admetus' life if someone else will die in his place. The only volunteer is his beautiful and loyal young wife, Alcestis. His father and mother, whom Admetus might have expected to volunteer, have refused the service. Thanetos – Death's messenger from Hades – has come to collect his victim. The whole household is in mourning. Alcestis has washed and dressed herself in her funeral garments. She has said her goodbyes to her young children and, already in the throes of death and sinking fast, she has come to say goodbye to her husband, supported by her grieving handmaidens.

Alcestis is a gracious, homely young queen who is loved by all for her gentleness, nobility and moderation. She is a good mother and a loving wife. Her love is expressed not through what she says – the word 'love' is never mentioned – but through the sacrifice she is making. The speech has been translated into beautifully balanced rhyming couplets, which give Alcestis' words a powerful simplicity. There is no recrimination. To die in place of her husband is the right and proper thing to do. To leave her children fatherless would be unthinkable. Alcestis is completely wrapped up in her family's welfare. She has only one request before she dies, that Admetus doesn't take another wife, for fear her children will be mistreated and the interests of her little daughter not attended to when she marries. Her concerns are tenderly addressed to Admetus through this child whom she is leaving behind. It is a heart-rending farewell to husband and family, all the more touching for the quiet, unquestioning acceptance of her fate.

This is a story with a happy ending, however. When the hero Heracles discovers what has happened, he rushes to

the vault where Alcestis has been buried. After doing battle
with Death itself, he reclaims her and returns her to an
overjoyed and chastened Admetus.

———————

Alcestis

Admetus, seeing what way my fortunes lie,
I would fain speak with thee before I die.
I have set thee before all things; yea, mine own
Life beside thine was naught. For this alone
I die . . . Dear Lord, I never need have died.
I might have lived to wed some prince of pride,
Dwell in a king's house . . . Nay, how could I, torn
From thee, live on, I and my babes forlorn?
I have given to thee my youth – not more nor less,
But all – though I was full of happiness.
Thy father and mother both – 'tis strange to tell –
Had failed thee, though for them the deed was well,
The years were ripe, to die and save their son,
The one child of the house: for hope was none,
If thou shouldst pass away, of other heirs.
So thou and I had lived through the long years,
Both. Thou hadst not lain sobbing here alone
For a dead wife and orphan babes . . . 'This done
Now, and some God hath wrought out all his will.

Howbeit I now will ask thee to fulfil
One great return-gift – not so great withal
As I have given, for life is more than all;
But just and due, as thine own heart will tell
For thou hast loved our little ones as well
As I have . . . Keep them to be masters here
In my old house; and bring no stepmother
Upon them. She might hate them. She might be
Some baser woman, not a queen like me,
And strike them with her hand. For mercy, spare
Our little ones that wrong. It is my prayer . . .
They come into a house: they are all strife
And hate to any child of the dead wife . . .
Better a serpent than a stepmother!

A boy is safe. He has his father there
To guard him. But a little girl! (*Taking the*

Little Girl *to her*.) What good
And gentle care will guide thy maidenhood?
What woman wilt thou find at father's side?
One evil word from her, just when the tide
Of youth is full, would wreck thy hope of love.
And no more mother near, to stand above
Thy marriage-bed, nor comfort thee pain-tossed
In travail, when one needs a mother most!
Seeing I must die . . . 'Tis here, across my way,
Not for the morrow, not for the third day,
But now – Death, and to lie with things that were.

Farewell. God keep you happy. – Husband dear,
Remember that I failed thee not; and you,
My children, that your mother loved you true.

Iphigeneia from *Iph . . .* after *Iphigenia in Aulis* by Euripides (adapted by Colin Teevan)

First performed in Athens in 405 BC, a couple of years after Euripides' death, *Iphigenia in Aulis* has since become one of the most performed of Greek tragedies. It explores the breakdown of social norms in times of war and how 'war breeds inhuman habits in the most humane of men' – a topic still relevant today. It dramatises the myth of Iphigeneia who was sacrificed by her father, Agamemnon, Commander-in-Chief of the Greek armies, to further his military ambitions, and questions how far an ambitious leader will go to save face and secure victory.

Agamemnon's fleet is stranded by bad weather in the bay of Aulis and his troops are growing mutinous. In revenge for Agamemnon killing one of her sacred stags, the goddess Artemis demands the sacrifice of his eldest daughter in return for a fair wind. Agamemnon summons Iphigeneia and her mother Klytaimnestra to Aulis under the pretext that she is to marry the Greek warrior Achilleus, but when they get there they learn Agamemnon has other plans.

Achilleus is outraged at having his name used to deceive Iphigeneia and vows to protect her. As Iphigeneia and her mother huddle in front of her father's quarters, a lynch mob approaches. In spite of Achilleus' brave determination to save her, it is clear the situation is hopeless. As the mob gets closer Achilleus and Klytaimnestra anxiously question what is to be done, but Iphigeneia, a naive virginal teenager, stops them in their tracks, suddenly announcing her resolve to embrace her fate. It is heartbreakingly simplistic, full of high-flown idealism, youthful vehemence and patriotic fervour. She is acting in accordance with what she regards as 'god's will' – in this case the will of Artemis – preparing to give her life for her country – rationalising that the success of her father's military campaign outweighs the importance of her own life. Perhaps her absence from Greece and the terrible situation she is in has heightened her allegiances.

18

Why Iphigeneia switches so suddenly from pleading for her life to embracing her death, from being a traumatised teenager to an idealistic martyr is a moot point, though Edith Hall's introduction to Colin Teevan's version shines some excellent light on the historical context.

Iphigeneia

Mother, Sir,
Please listen to my words.
In vain you try to save me.
It is a fearful thing indeed
To face up to the unfaceable.
But we must.
It is right, Mother, that you praise this man,
But you know we cannot hope to win.
So realise his fameglory
Will be damaged in defending us.

Listen to these words I have to say:
As I've been standing here I've thought,
Thought of that which is being asked of me,
And have decided I must die.
Die for Greece, die for her hero men,
Die famously and freely,
Die by my own consent
With no shallow thoughts of self.
See now how well I speak?

To me all Greece now looks in hope;
To me it lies to launch
Our shining ships on Troy;
To me it now falls to keep
Barbarians from our land.
And by my blood
I'll help to pay back
Paris for his rape.
I must serve Greece,
And so win my own fameglory.
It is not right for one like me
To love this life too much.
Our lives should not be lived
For just ourselves alone.

I was born for Greece not for myself.
Myriad men stand ready armed,
Myriad more sit at their oars;
Greece has been sore wronged
And these Greeks would gladly die
For their beloved homeland.
How can I cry out, 'No,
I do not want to die'?
It is not right.
Nor is it right that Achilleus
Might lose his life for mine;
A warman's life is of more use
For our homeland's cause.
And furthermore, how can mortals
Reject what great Artemis demands?
I have no choice, so choose to die.
Sacrifice me, then smash Troy;
Smash Troy and all those stinking Trojans!
That will be memorial enough.
Women will sing my glory evermore.
It is right we rule Barbarians,
For we are free and they are not.

Zenocrate from *Tamburlaine the Great* by Christopher Marlowe

This play – written in two five-act parts – was first performed in London in 1587 and was possibly the opening production at the new Rose Theatre. Its heroic theme centres on the fourteenth-century Mogul conqueror, Tamburlaine, whose relentless rise to power and enormous greed and vanity resulted in his downfall.

Tamburlaine is a man of lowly birth, an 'outsider' who sets out to conquer the Eastern world and win the love of 'the divine' Zenocrate, daughter of the Sultan of Egypt – 'Zenocrate, the loveliest maid alive / Fairer than rocks of pearl and precious stone' – whom he captures on a military raid. Tamburlaine promptly falls in love with her and determines to make her his empress. Having seized Zenocrate he goes on to conquer Persia and Turkey and puts Damascus to the sword, slaughtering its citizens, displaying the speared carcasses of virgins on the city walls and throwing the Turkish Emperor, Bajezeth, into a public cage to humiliate him in front of his followers. Rather than be Tamburlaine's slave, Bajezeth hurls himself against the bars of the cage and brains himself, and when his grief-stricken Empress finds him, she does the same. By this time Zenocrate is as much in love with Tamburlaine as he with her.

Here, Zenocrate comes across the bloody scene of the double suicide and gives voice to this eloquent, 'chorus-like' lament, juxtaposed with its haunting refrain 'Behold the Turk and his great emperess'. This is Marlowe the poet using his considerable gifts to offer up Zenocrate's respectful pity for the fallen Emperor and Empress on our behalf, while at the same time asking the gods to forgive Tamburlaine for his ruthless pursuit of 'scepters and slippery crowns' – begging them not to visit a similar fate on him.

The regular pulse of the metre counterpointed with the dirge-like refrain seems to give epic weight to the powerful and conflicted emotions Zenocrate expresses. This is one of the great 'set pieces' of the play with its ringing final question about what fate might have in store for her.

Zenocrate

Earth, cast up fountains from thy entrails,
And wet thy cheeks for their untimely deaths;
Shake with their weight in sign of fear and grief.
Blush, heaven, that gave them honor at their birth
And let them die a death so barbarous.
Those that are proud of fickle empery
And place their chiefest good in earthly pomp,
Behold the Turk and his great emperess!
Ah, Tamburlaine, my love, sweet Tamburlaine,
That fights for scepters and for slippery crowns,
Behold the Turk and his great emperess!
Thou that in conduct of thy happy stars
Sleep'st every night with conquest on thy brows,
And yet wouldst shun the wavering turns of war,
In fear and feeling of the like distress,
Behold the Turk and his great emperess!
Ah, mighty Jove and holy Mahomet,
Pardon my love! O, pardon his contempt
Of earthly fortune and respect of pity,
And let not conquest, ruthlessly pursu'd,
Be equally against his life incens'd
In this great Turk and hapless emperess!
And pardon me that was not mov'd with ruth
To see them live so long in misery.
Ah, what may chance to thee, Zenocrate?

---

in conduct: under the guidance
and respect: and of consideration
in: as in
ruth: pity

Alice Arden from *Arden of Feversham* (anon)

This domestic tragicomedy, published in 1592, is based on a notorious real-life murder committed in 1551 – 'the lamentable and true tragedy of master Arden of Feversham in Kent who was most wickedly murdered by the means of his disloyal and wanton wife who, for the love she bore to one Mosbie, hired two desperate ruffians Black Will and Shakebag to kill him'. It is an action-packed tale of strong passions, class envy, murder and greed.

Alice Arden, Thomas Arden's murderous wife, is described in contemporary records as 'a tall and comely person . . . a gentlewoman, who was young, well shaped, and every way handsome'. Our anonymous author characterises her as a compelling, assertive, plausible woman with considerable powers of persuasion. She has fallen for Mosbie, an ambitious man from the working class. Driven by desire for Mosbie and hatred of her husband, she determines to murder him with Mosbie as her accomplice. She is like a small-town Lady Macbeth instructing her man to carry out her violent demands. (Shakespeare has, in fact, been suggested as the play's author.)

At this point Mosbie has suffered a panic attack of conscience and has been drinking. He doesn't trust Alice and even contemplates doing away with her once Arden is dead. He accuses her of manipulating his emotions. She in turn accuses him of bewitching her and destroying her marriage. He hits back by saying it is he who was bewitched and that he now sees her in her true colours. This speech comes in the middle of their lovers' quarrel. Both are feeling the pressure but Mosbie is no match for his quick-thinking, silver-tongued mistress who winds him round her little finger, employing all her womanly wiles to patch things up between them. She takes the blame for the things that have gone wrong between them, saying how good they are together, how much she values his love letters, how life is not worth living without him, arguing that he is not thinking clearly and she will only take him seriously when he is. Mosbie gives in to her persuasive charms and the couple are reconciled.

Alice

Ay, now I see, and too soon find it true,
Which often hath been told me by my friends,
That Mosbie loves me not but for my wealth,
Which too incredulous I ne'er believ'd.
Nay, hear me speak, Mosbie, a word or two;
I'll bite my tongue if it speak bitterly.
Look on me, Mosbie, or I'll kill myself:
Nothing shall hide me from thy stormy look.
If thou cry war, there is no peace for me;
I will do penance for offending thee,
And burn this prayer-book, where I here see
The holy word that had converted me.
See, Mosbie, I will tear away the leaf,
And all the leaves, and in this golden cover
Shall thy sweet phrases and thy letters dwell;
And thereon will I chiefly meditate,
And hold no other sect but such devotion.
Wilt thou not look? is all thy love o'erwhelm'd?
Wilt thou not hear? what malice stops thine ears?
Why speaks thou not? what silence ties thy tongue?
Thou hast been sighted as the eagle is,
And heard as quickly as the fearful hare,
And spoke as smoothly as an orator,
When I have bid thee hear or see or speak,
And art thou sensible in none of these?
Weigh all thy good turns with this little fault,
And I deserve not Mosbie's muddy looks.
A fount once troubl'd is not thicken'd still:
Be clear again, I'll ne'er more trouble thee.

Titania from *A Midsummer Night's Dream* by William Shakespeare

A comedy written around 1595, the action takes place on midsummer's eve, a customary time for strange and magical events. It moves between Athens and a nearby wood during the preparations for the marriage of Duke Theseus and Hippolyta. Several plots interweave involving four lovers, preparations for the wedding entertainment by local workmen, and a quarrel between Oberon, King of the Fairies, and his imperious, supernatural Queen, Titania, who rule the mysterious twilight world of the woods.

Their quarrel is over a little changeling boy in Titania's entourage whom Oberon wants as his page. Titania has refused to hand him over and the couple have fallen out. In this scene Titania bumps into Oberon in the moonlit wood. She quickly dispatches her fairy attendants and the couple waste no time in hurling insults and accusations at each other about having affairs – Titania with Theseus and Oberon with Hippolyta – and Titania claiming Oberon is inventing things because he is jealous that she has the boy.

Titania is used to having her own way. She is not governed by human morality. She can change shape and location, become invisible, move at the speed of light and change the course of love and the workings of nature. Nevertheless, she is not above displays of human emotion and these are very much in evidence here. She is not prepared to give an inch and blames Oberon for a catalogue of disasters, accusing him of disrupting her fairy business with his ranting and turning everything upside down. In some of the most powerful and poetic language in the play she describes a frightening disruption of the natural world – disastrous floods, failing crops, starving animals and ruined blossom – a world in which poor humans no longer know which season is which – disruptive primal forces mirroring the couple's disharmony. The imagery is vivid. The seasons and elements are invested with human qualities. The wind is vengeful. The moon is angry. The autumn chides. The world is bewildered (mazèd). Titania blames everything on their abdication of responsibility and doesn't give the furious Oberon the chance to get a word in edgeways. When he finally does manage to suggest the solution lies in her own hands, she flounces off without giving him any satisfaction, and he is left to devise more cunning strategies to get his own way.

Titania

These are the forgeries of jealousy;
And never since the middle summer's spring
Met we on hill, in dale, forest, or mead,
By pavèd fountain or by rushy brook,
Or in the beachèd margent of the sea
To dance our ringlets to the whistling wind,
But with thy brawls thou hast disturbed our sport.
Therefore the winds, piping to us in vain,
As in revenge have sucked up from the sea
Contagious fogs which, falling in the land,
Hath every pelting river made so proud
That they have overborne their continents.
The ox hath therefore stretched his yoke in vain,
The ploughman lost his sweat, and the green corn
Hath rotted ere his youth attained a beard.
The fold stands empty in the drownèd field,
And crows are fatted with the murrion flock.
The nine men's morris is filled up with mud,
And the quaint mazes in the wanton green
For lack of tread are undistinguishable.
The human mortals want their winter cheer.
No night is now with hymn or carol blessed.
Therefore the moon, the governess of floods,
Pale in her anger, washes all the air,
That rheumatic diseases do abound;
And thorough this distemperature we see
The seasons alter; hoary-headed frosts
Fall in the fresh lap of the crimson rose,
And on old Hiems' thin and icy crown
An odorous chaplet of sweet summer buds
Is as in mockery set. The spring, the summer,
The childing autumn, angry winter change
Their wonted liveries, and the mazèd world
By their increase now knows not which is which.
And this same progeny of evils

Comes from our debate, from our dissension.
We are their parents and original.

---

pavèd: pebbled
ringlets: dances in a circle
pelting: paltry
continents: banks
murrion flock: diseased animals
nine men's morris: an open-air game using squares marked on the ground
quaint mazes: intricate footpaths
wanton green: thick grass
rheumatic: coughs and colds
Hiems: the personification of winter
childing: fruitful
wonted: usual
mazèd: amazed or bewildered
increase: seasonal produce

Portia from *Julius Caesar* by William Shakespeare

Julius Caesar is probably the earliest of Shakespeare's Roman history plays, the others being *Antony and Cleopatra* and *Coriolanus*. Its first performance was around 1599, shortly after the completion of the Globe.

The play opens with Caesar's triumphal return from various civil wars and a rejoicing crowd attempting to crown him as King. They treat him like a god, but a group of Roman generals are less convinced of his suitability for the crown. Even his close friend Brutus is concerned that Caesar is unstable and becoming too powerful. A conspiracy is hatched between the generals to remove Caesar from power. They meet under cover of darkness at Brutus' house and decide Caesar must die. Brutus agrees to be part of the plan for the most patriotic of motives, in spite of his love for Caesar.

Portia is a proud and courageous noblewoman who has been married to Brutus for some years. She has seen the hooded conspirators in her garden, so she suspects something covert and dangerous is going on. After the conspirators have gone, Brutus can't sleep and Portia wakes to find him wandering outside in the chilly early-morning air. Brutus claims he is feeling unwell, but Portia has already noticed his agitated state of mind and doesn't believe him. If he is ill then it is absurd that he should be outside in the freezing cold in his nightclothes, she argues. She pleads with him to confide in her and share his troubles, calling upon her status as a loyal wife and claiming that her noble breeding places her above other women in fortitude and qualifies her for equal status in their relationship. To treat her otherwise is to treat her as a whore. Powerful words from a woman who knows the noble nature of her husband well. As further evidence of her loyalty and discretion and as proof she can suffer anything her husband can suffer, she has stabbed herself in the thigh – a painful wound she bears without complaint. Could there be any more persuasive indicators of the depth of her anxiety and strength of her commitment?

A loud knocking interrupts them and Portia goes, but not
before Brutus has promised to reveal all.

———————————

Portia

Is Brutus sick? and is it physical
To walk unbraced, and suck up the humours
Of the dank morning? What, is Brutus sick, –
And will he steal out of his wholesome bed,
To dare the vile contagion of the night,
And tempt the rheumy and unpurg'd air
To add unto his sickness? No, my Brutus;
You have some sick offence within your mind,
Which by the right and virtue of my place
I ought to know of: and upon my knees
I charm you, by my once-commended beauty,
By all your vows of love, and that great vow
Which did incorporate and make us one,
That you unfold to me, yourself, your half,
Why you are heavy; and what men to-night
Have had resort to you, – for here have been
Some six or seven, who did hide their faces
Even from darkness.
Within the bond of marriage, tell me, Brutus,
Is it excepted I should know no secrets.
That appertain to you? Am I yourself
But as it were in sort or limitation, –
To keep with you at meals, comfort your bed,
And talk to you sometimes? Dwell I but in the suburbs
Of your good pleasure? If it be no more,
Portia is Brutus' harlot, not his wife.
I grant I am a woman; but withal
A woman that Lord Brutus took to wife:
I grant I am a woman; but withal
A woman well-reputed, – Cato's daughter.
Think you I am no stronger than my sex,
Being so father'd and so husbanded?
Tell me your counsels, I will not disclose 'em:
I have made strong proof of my constancy,
Giving myself a voluntary wound

Here in the thigh: can I bear that with patience,
And not my husband's secrets?

Celia from *Volpone* by Ben Jonson

First performed in 1605, *Volpone* is appropriately set in Venice, considered to be the throbbing heart of opulence and debauchery in the seventeenth century, and is a satire on greed and lust in a money-obsessed society.

A rich and childless nobleman, Volpone, and his parasitic lackey, Mosca, conspire to swindle three avaricious bounty hunters, each of whom wants to be Volpone's sole heir. In a well-planned scam, Volpone pretends to be on his deathbed so they will shower him with expensive presents to win his favour and, subsequently, his ill-gotten fortune.

Celia, the virtuous young wife of the bounty hunter Corvino, has been described by Mosca as one of the most beautiful women in Italy. Her jealous husband keeps her guarded under lock and key, but inflamed by Mosca's luminous description, and a brief sighting, Volpone determines to have her by any means. Mosca convinces Corvino that if he allows Celia to lie next to the dying man, it will encourage Volpone to name him as sole heir and probably bring about his early death. Corvino is persuaded and a terrified Celia is dragged into Volpone's sickroom. The moment she is left alone Volpone leaps from his 'deathbed' and makes his play, courting her with the most compelling language. The terrified Celia pleads with him to preserve her honour in a fruitless appeal to his better nature. Shamed and 'prostituted' by her husband's behaviour, she is prepared to suffer anything – even death, mutilation – rather than be dishonoured. But the licentious Volpone is not to be deterred.

Jonson's characters are 'types' that his audiences could recognise (Volpone the fox, Mosca the fly, Corvino the raven) and Celia conforms to the pious young wife stereotype. She is the voice of goodness and piety in the play – yet she has backbone too as she makes this spirited defence of her honour in the face of her husband's demands. It is your challenge to make her more than a flat and predictable cipher.

Celia

Good sir, these things might move a mind affected
With such delights; but I, whose innocence
Is all I can think wealthy or worth th' enjoying,
And which, once lost, I have nought to lose beyond it,
Cannot be taken with these sensual baits:
If you have conscience –
If you have ears that will be pierced; or eyes
That can be opened; a heart that may be touched;
Or any part that yet sounds man about you:
If you have touch of holy saints, or heaven,
Do me the grace to let me 'scape. If not,
Be bountiful, and kill me. You do know
I am a creature hither ill-betrayed
By one whose shame I would forget it were.
If you will deign me neither of these graces,
Yet feed your wrath, sir, rather than your lust
(It is a vice comes nearer manliness)
And punish that unhappy crime of Nature
Which you miscall my beauty: flay my face,
Or poison it with ointments, for seducing
Your blood in this rebellion. Rub these hands
With what may cause an eating leprosy
E'en to my bones and marrow; anything
That may disfavour me, save in my honour.
And I will kneel to you, pray for you, pay down
A thousand hourly vows, sir, for your health;
Report and think you virtuous –
Oh! just God!

Mistress Milligrub from *The Dutch Courtesan* by John Marston

This comedy – written in 1605 – was reportedly first performed before the court of James I in 1613. It is a tale of virgins and whores, love and lust, double-dealing, trickery and disguise moving between the lower and upper stratas of society in the vibrant cityscape of an increasingly commercial Jacobean London.

A comic sub-plot charts the intrigues of a conman, Cocledemoy, to expose and punish the pretensions of a swindling 'puritanical' publican Mulligrub.

Mistress Mulligrub is the publican's wife, a silly, bourgeois, garrulous woman with social-climbing pretensions. The couple run a dubious business, 'cooking the books', profiteering, mixing water with the wine and turning a blind eye to the use of their tavern by undesirables.

Here, she is talking to Lionel, manservant to Burnish, a goldsmith who has sold them a goblet (on a promise payment as they don't have the money) to replace a plate stolen by Cocledemoy as a prank. Mistress Mulligrub knows she is now in Burnish's debt but is still anxious to hang on to her status in front of a servant. She does this by using an affected and over-civil vocabulary, claiming a long and intimate acquaintance with the Burnishes (a particularly close one in the case of Mr Burnish) and overpraising their business skills. Even though Mrs Burnish has come up in the world and 'paints' she hasn't lost the common touch! All empty flattery shot through with envy, and she can't resist making snide sexual innuendos about both of them.

The moment Lionel leaves, the 'proper' tone is dropped as she reassures herself that she has behaved with appropriate civility. She is as good as any of them 'by association'. After all, who is relied on for credit? Who gets rewarded by seasonal game? Not her 'cloth-capped' husband! No, she is the brains behind the business. In truth she is all prattle, pretension and posturing, easily flattered and tricked by anyone above her station.

Mistress Mulligrub Nay, I pray you, stay and drink. And how does your mistress? I know her very well; I have been inward with her, and so has many more. She was ever a good, patient creature, i' faith. With all my heart, I'll remember your master, an honest man; he knew me before I was married. An honest man he is, and a crafty. He comes forward in the world well, I warrant him; and his wife is a proper woman, that she is. Well, she has been as proper a woman as any in Cheap; she paints now, and yet she keeps her husband's old customers to him still. In troth, a fine-fac'd wife in a wainscot carved seat is a worthy ornament to a tradesman's shop, and an attractive, I warrant; her husband shall find it in the custom of his ware, I'll assure him. God be with you, good youth. I acknowledge the receipt. (*Exit* **Lionel**.) I acknowledge all the receipt – sure, 'tis very well spoken! I acknowledge the receipt! Thus 'tis to have good education and to be brought up in a tavern. I do keep as gallant and as good company, though I say it, as any she in London. Squires, gentlemen, and knights diet at my table, and I do lend some of them money; and full many fine men go upon my score, as simple as I stand here, and I trust them; and truly they very knightly and courtly promise fair, give me very good words, and a piece of flesh when time of year serves. Nay, though my husband be a citizen and's cap's made of wool, yet I ha' wit and can see my good as soon as another; for I have all the thanks. My silly husband, alas, he knows nothing of it; 'tis I that bear – 'tis I that must bear a brain for all.

---

inward: intimate (with sexual innuendo following)
knew me: in the biblical sense
Cheap: Cheapside
paints: applies make-up
score: accounts
and's cap's made of wool: a 'flat-cap' was a pejorative name for a tradesman

Duchess from *The Revenger's Tragedy*
attributed to Cyril Tourner

The Revenger's Tragedy, first published anonymously in 1607, is thought to have been written by Cyril Tourneur or maybe Thomas Middleton. A gruesome mix of jealousy, lust, incest, fratricide, rape, adultery and multiple murder set in decadent Renaissance Italy, it is a revenge tragedy of such blood-curdling decadence it is almost a parody of itself.

It begins with Vindice (his name means vengeance) addressing the skull of his beloved Gloriana who has been poisoned by the lecherous old Duke for not succumbing to his advances. He is intent on avenging her death. Meanwhile, the Duchess's son Junior (the Duke's stepson) has been accused of raping the pious wife of a nobleman who has committed suicide and the Duke has condemned him to death.

The Duchess begs for her son's life, but her pleas are ignored and Junior is led off under suspended sentence leaving the Duchess alone and filled with loathing for her despotic old husband. Junior is her youngest, best-loved son, but the Duke would not relent. She knows any challenge to the Duke's authority is dangerous so she appears cool and collected in his presence. A clever and considered public strategy. Now she is alone we become privy to her darker thoughts.

The Duchess is a lascivious, resourceful, persuasive and calculating dowager – not unattractive for her age – a cool customer who will bide her time. Coldly and dispassionately she considers the options for revenge on the Duke, rejecting ideas of plotting his death in favour of a more painful psychological solution.

The Duchess has three sons from a previous marriage, the Duke has one bastard son, Spurio, who hates him. She is intent on seducing Spurio, courting him with letters and jewels. So far her efforts have fallen on stony ground, but the Duchess is not one to be deterred. To cuckold the Duke with his own son would be the sweetest and most appropriate revenge. She turns on all her womanly charms as Spurio approaches.

Duchess

Was't ever known step-Duchess was so mild
And calm as I? Some now would plot his death
With easy doctors, those loose-living men,
And make his withered Grace fall to his grave
And keep church better.
Some second wife would do this, and dispatch
Her double-loathéd lord at meat, and sleep.
Indeed 'tis true an old man's twice a child;
Mind cannot speak, one of his single words
Would quite have freed my youngest dearest son
From death or durance, and have made him walk
With a bold foot upon the thorny law
Whose prickles should bow under him; but 'tis not,
And therefore wedlock faith shall be forgot;
I'll kill him in his forehead, hate there feed,
That wound is deepest, tho' it never bleed.
(*Enter* **Spurio**.)
And here comes he whom my heart points unto,
His bastard son, but my love's true-begot;
Many a wealthy letter have I sent him
Swelled up with jewels, and the timorous man
Is yet but coldly kind;
That jewel's mine that quivers in his ear
Mocking his master's chillness and vain fear.
H'as spied me now.

Bianca from *Women Beware Women* by Thomas Middleton

Written in the early 1600s, this is a violent Jacobean tragedy – a complex tale of murder, lechery, revenge, rape and incest based on real historical events in sixteenth-century Italy.

Bianca is a beautiful, innocent Venetian aged sixteen who has left her controlling family, 'forsaken friends, fortunes and her country', to marry Leantio, a Florentine merchant's clerk who is much below her station. Once married Leantio seems more preoccupied with his business affairs than his young wife. She is a vulnerable newcomer, 'a stranger', in Florence and her youth and beauty quickly attract the libidinous attentions of the middle-aged Duke. In the hope of future riches and advancement, Livia, a wealthy widow, and her co-conspirator, Guardiano, plot to deliver her up to him. Posing as Bianca's friends and confidantes, they lure her and her mother-in-law to Livia's house and while the hostess distracts the mother-in-law with a game of chess, Guardiano conducts Bianca to Livia's gallery, then abandons her to the lustful advances of the waiting Duke who effectively rapes her with an explosive mix of force, threats, calculated charm and the seductive offer of wealth and security.

While Guardiano congratulates himself on their success, Bianca contemplates her dishonour. She lays a curse on Guardiano for his treachery, yet she appears emboldened by her new situation. Everything on offer from the Duke – wealth, honour, glory – is attractive to her. She calculates the benefits of her new situation against the loss of her innocence (as Livia says at the end of the scene 'Sin tastes at first like wormwood water / But drunk again, 'tis nectar ever after') and begins to see the advantages of being the mistress of a duke and ironically thanks Guardiano. Quite a change from the demeanour of the virtuous newlywed at the beginning of the play. Look how she demotes Guardiano to 'slave' at the end of the speech, as if already embracing her elevated social status.

Bianca (*aside*)

Now bless me from a blasting; I saw that now
Fearful for any woman's eye to look on.
Infectious mists and mildews hang at 's eyes,
The weather of a doomsday dwells upon him.
Yet since mine honour's leprous, why should I
Preserve that fair that caused the leprosy?
Come poison all at once. (*Aside to* **Guardiano**.) Thou in whose
   baseness
The bane of virtue broods, I'm bound in soul
Eternally to curse thy smooth-browed treachery,
That wore the fair veil of a friendly welcome,
And I a stranger; think upon 't, 'tis worth it.
Murders piled up upon a guilty spirit
At his last breath will not lie heavier
Than this betraying act upon thy conscience.
Beware of off'ring the first-fruits to sin:
His weight is deadly, who commits with strumpets
After they have been abased, and made for us;
If they offend to th' death, as wise men know,
How much more they then that first make 'em so?
I give thee that to feed on. I'm made bold now;
I thank thy treachery, sin and I'm acquainted,
No couple greater. And I'm like that great one
Who making politic use of a base villain,
He likes the treason well, but hates the traitor.
So I hate thee, slave.

---

blasting: moral infection caught from the Duke
leprous/leprosy: a metaphor for moral foulness
His weight is deadly . . . that first make 'em so: Bianca is saying that the 'strumpet maker' is far guiltier than those who use them

41

Queen Katharine from *Henry VIII* by William Shakespeare

The premiere of this history play in 1613 resulted in the burning down of the Globe Theatre, thanks to the 'special effects'. It is less frequently performed than many in the Shakespeare canon, being considered of doubtful authenticity and unfairly dismissed as 'pageantry'. Nevertheless, it has some splendid speeches in it.

Katharine of Aragon, Henry VIII's first wife, was a Spaniard. The daughter of Ferdinand, King of Spain, she was originally married to Henry's brother, Arthur – a match arranged to cement an alliance with Spain against France. Arthur died five months later and shortly afterwards Katharine married Henry. Their marriage lasted over twenty years until Henry, desperate for a male heir, no longer needing Spain as an ally and – more to the point – being infatuated by Katharine's pretty maid of honour, Anne Boleyn, wanted a divorce. Katharine, a devout Catholic, refused to give it to him. Henry, pleading a rather belated attack of conscience for marrying his brother's wife, sought the support of his close adviser Cardinal Wolsey, to intercede with the Pope on the legality of his marriage.

In this scene, Katharine has been arraigned before her husband and the Grand Court of Bishops for judgement on the matter. Henry's displeasure has left her isolated and friendless – suddenly very much a foreigner. She kneels before Henry like a humble petitioner, knowing she will not get a fair hearing from Wolsey, with whom she has already crossed swords.

Katharine is a pious, shrewd and dignified Queen, now in late middle age and no longer beautiful. She has been a good and faithful wife to Henry and she still loves him. This is an appeal from the heart of a wife to a husband – a woman who has borne his children, suffered their loss in infancy and been beyond reproach in love, duty and obedience. She knows her behaviour has been irreproachable and she appeals to Henry's better instincts to save her from the foregone conclusion of the Court.

Queen Katharine

Sir, I desire you do me right and justice;
And to bestow your pity on me: for
I am a most poor woman, and a stranger,
Born out of your dominions; having here
No judge indifferent, nor no more assurance
Of equal friendship and proceeding. Alas, sir,
In what have I offended you? what cause
Hath my behaviour given to your displeasure,
That thus you should proceed to put me off,
And take your good grace from me? Heaven witness,
I have been to you a true and humble wife,
At all times to your will conformable:
Ever in fear to kindle your dislike,
Yea, subject to your countenance, – glad or sorry
As I saw it inclin'd. When was the hour
I ever contradicted your desire,
Or made it not mine too? Or which of your friends
Have I not strove to love, although I knew
He were mine enemy? what friend of mine
That had to him deriv'd your anger, did I
Continue in my liking? nay, gave notice
He was from thence discharg'd? Sir, call to mind
That I have been your wife, in this obedience,
Upward of twenty years, and have been blest
With many children by you: if, in the course
And process of this time, you can report,
And prove it too, against mine honour aught,
My bond to wedlock or my love and duty,
Against your sacred person, in God's name,
Turn me away; and let the foul'st contempt
Shut door upon me, and so give me up
To the sharp'st kind of justice.

Beatrice-Joanna from *The Changeling* by Thomas Middleton and William Rowley

The Changeling (one who is not what he or she appears to be) was written in 1622 and is regarded as one of the masterpieces of Jacobean theatre. Set in Catholic Spain, it is a typically gory tragedy about obsessive passion, male domination, murder, revenge and moral decay.

The play's anti-heroine, Beatrice-Joanna, is the daughter of Vermandero, governor of Alicante. She is spoilt, self-obsessed, high-born, beautiful, wilful, completely immoral and used to exercising her rank to get her way. Vermandero has promised Beatrice-Joanna to a young nobleman, Alonzo, with little regard for her happiness, but Beatrice-Joanna is in love with Alsemero, another nobleman. Driven by lust for Alsemero, desperate to be rid of Alonzo yet appear the chaste and dutiful daughter, she conspires with her father's repulsive servant De Flores to kill him, but after the murder, he hides the body and demands her virginity as a reward. Repelled at having placed herself at his mercy and having brought herself down to his level, she submits, then rather perversely continues their sexual relationship.

Act 4 begins on the day of Beatrice Beatrice-Joanna's wedding to Alsemero. While he is in the park, she creeps into his room and gains access to a secret cupboard. Beatrice-Joanna knows how much Alsemero values chastity in a wife and is afraid he will discover her infidelity on their wedding night.

In this soliloquy she blames De Flores for her situation. This is a cunning mind at work. Beatrice-Joanna is less consumed by guilt than by how to cover her tracks and escape discovery. As she rifles through the contents of Alsemero's cabinet, each find confirms Alsemero's preoccupations and suspicions and the danger she is in if he finds out she is not a virgin. Among the hard evidence of his obsessions are books containing pregnancy tests, potions and experiments to test purity. Maybe she is already pregnant? What if he finds her out? How can she use this knowledge to her advantage? She has seven hours in which to find a solution, which comes in the shape of her chaste maid, Diaphanta, whom she bribes to take her place in the bridal bed, with fatal consequences.

———————

Beatrice-Joanna

This fellow has undone me endlessly,
Never was bride so fearfully distress'd;
The more I think upon th' ensuing night,
And whom I am to cope with in embraces,
One who's ennobled both in blood and mind,
So clear in understanding, – that's my plague now –
Before whose judgement will my fault appear
Like malefactors' crimes before tribunals;
There is no hiding on't, the more I dive
Into my own distress; how a wise man
Stands for a great calamity! There's no venturing
Into his bed, what course soe'er I light upon,
Without my shame, which may grow up to danger;
He cannot but in justice strangle me
As I lie by him, as a cheater use me;
'Tis a precious craft to play with a false die
Before a cunning gamester. Here's his closet,
The key left in't, and he abroad i'th' park.
Sure 'twas forgot; I'll be so bold as to look in't. (*Opens closet.*)
Bless me! A right physician's closet 'tis,
Set round with vials, every one her mark too.
Sure he does practise physic for his own use,
Which may be safely call'd your great man's wisdom.
What manuscript lies here? 'The Book of Experiment,
Call'd Secrets in Nature'; so 'tis, 'tis so;
'How to know whether a woman be with child or no';
I hope I am not yet; if he should try though!
Let me see, folio forty-five. Here 'tis;
The leaf ruck'd down upon't, the place suspicious:
'If you would know whether a woman be with child or not, give
her two spoonfuls of the white water in glass C' –
Where's that glass C? Oh, yonder, I see't now – 'and if she be with
child she sleeps full twelve hours after; if not, not.'
None of that water comes into my belly.
I'll know you from a hundred; I could break you now,

Or turn you into milk, and so beguile
The master of the mystery, but I'll look to you.
Ha. That which is next is ten times worse:
'How to know whether a woman be a maid or not.'
If that should be appli'd, what would become of me?
Belike he has a strong faith of my purity,
That never yet made proof; but this he calls
'A merry sleight, but true experiment, the author Antonius
Mizaldus. Give the party you suspect the quantity of a spoonful of
the water in the glass M, which, upon her that is a maid, makes
three several effects: 'twill make her incontinently gape, then fall
into a sudden sneezing, last into a violent laughing; else dull,
heavy, and lumpish.'
Where had I been?
I fear it, yet 'tis seven hours to bedtime.

---

gamester: rake
incontinently: immediately

Penthea from *The Broken Heart* by John Ford

The Broken Heart, written between 1625 and 1634, is the least known of Ford's plays. Set in Sparta, its theme is the conflict between love and duty and the tragic consequences of an enforced marriage.

The play opens with the nobleman Orgilus (meaning 'angry') telling his father of his plans to study in Athens. His pre-marriage contract to his beloved Penthea ('compliant') has been broken off by her brother and she has been forced to marry Bassanes instead. His voluntary exile is to save Penthea more pain and protect her integrity – a gesture that doesn't last long. Against all wise advice, he disguises himself as a scholar so he can stay in Sparta, keeping watch and planning revenge.

Penthea is on the horns of a desperate dilemma. At first she appears dutiful to Bassanes despite her love for Orgilus, but the conflict between appearing a virtuous wife and staying true to the man she loves causes increasing emotional turmoil – a 'divorce between her body and her heart'.

Here, Penthea has been decoyed into the garden and comes face to face with Orgilus who, to her consternation, throws off his disguise to claim her as his 'wife'. Her dilemma is made flesh. How can she be anything to Orgilus now she is married to Bassanes? She renounces Orgilus immediately and orders him to resume his disguise, but he persists in his claim to her love. His declaration threatens her honour, which she fiercely defends. In this speech she challenges the quality of a love that would place her reputation and his own in such jeopardy. By sending Orgilus away – telling him that his presence makes a bad situation worse, demanding that he never touches her, contacts her or writes to her again – she acts with self-sacrifice and because he loves her there is no further argument.

It is only when a distraught Orgilus leaves and she hears him cry her name that the mood changes and we see how tender her feelings are towards him and how much her rejection has cost.

Penthea

    Should I outlive my bondage, let me meet
    Another worse than this, and less desired,
    If, of all men alive, thou shouldst but touch
    My lip or hand again.
                     Uncivil sir, forbear,
    Or I can turn affection into vengeance;
    Your reputation (if you value any)
    Lies bleeding at my feet. Unworthy man,
    If ever henceforth thou appear in language,
    Message, or letter, to betray my frailty,
    I'll call thy former protestations lust,
    And curse my stars for forfeit of my judgement.
    Go thou, fit only for disguise and walks,
    To hide thy shame; this once I spare thy life.
    I laugh at mine own confidence; my sorrows
    By thee are made inferior to my fortunes.
    If ever thou didst harbour worthy love,
    Dare not to answer. My good genius guide me,
    That I may never see thee more. – Go from me.
    (*Exit* **Orgilus**.)
    'A sighed my name, sure, as he parted from me;
    I fear I was too rough. Alas, poor gentleman.
    'A looked not like the ruins of his youth,
    But like the ruins of those ruins. Honour,
    How much we fight with weakness to preserve thee.

Putana from *'Tis Pity She's a Whore* by John Ford

Ford's reputation rests largely on this play. It was first published in 1633, but because of its affinity to Jacobean revenge tragedies like *The Duchess of Malfi*, some think it was written much earlier. Set in Parma, in the bustling domestic environment of mercantile society, it addresses themes of lust, vengeance, greed and the controversial issue of incestuous love that finally pulls everyone's world apart.

Annabella, the 'whore' of the title, is the beautiful and much sought after young daughter of Florio, a well-heeled, middle-class citizen of Parma, who is keen for her to marry. In this scene, Annabella and her governess Putana (Italian for whore) have just witnessed an argument and the ensuing fight under Annabella's balcony between two rival suitors – Grimaldi, a Roman gentleman, and Vasques, a servant, who has been fighting on behalf of his master, Soranzo, the nobleman whom Annabella's father intends for her husband.

Putana is a bustling, gossipy, bawdy old tittle-tattle who takes a real maternal interest in marrying off her charge to the most suitable contender. Annabella's mother is dead and her only source of moral support is Putana, who adores her and protects her interests like a mother hen. She is much exercised over the matter of Annabella's choice of suitor and impressed that Annabella should have men fighting over her. Here she prattles on about the relative attributes of the two main contenders. There is no question about which gentleman Putana favours and she makes no bones about championing Soranzo, who is not only young and handsome, but rich as well! She makes the odd observation about their sexual capabilities too. But Annabella shows no interest in discussing sex, marriage or men, until her distraught brother Giovanni comes into view. When he tells her about his feelings and she tells him they are reciprocated the scene is set for the play's bloody and vengeful aftermath.

Putana How like you this, child? Here's threatening, challenging, quarrelling, and fighting, on every side, and all is for your sake; you had need look to yourself, charge, you'll be stolen away sleeping else shortly. Indeed I blame you not, you have choice fit for the best lady in Italy. Take the worst with the best, there's Grimaldi the soldier, a very well-timbered fellow. They say he is a Roman, nephew to the Duke Montferrato, they say he did good service in the wars against the Milanese, but 'faith, charge, I do not like him, an't be for nothing but for being a soldier; not one amongst twenty of your skirmishing captains but have some privy maim or other that mars their standing upright. I like him the worse, he crinkles so much in the hams; though he might serve if there were no more men, yet he's not the man I would choose. As I am a very woman, I like Signor Soranzo well; he is wise, and what is more, rich; and what is more than that, kind, and what is more than all this, a nobleman; such a one, were I the fair Annabella myself, I would wish and pray for. Then he is bountiful; besides, he is handsome, and by my troth, I think wholesome (and that's news in a gallant of three and twenty); liberal, that I know; loving, that you know; and a man sure, else he could never ha' purchased such a good name with Hippolita, the lusty widow, in her husband's lifetime: and 'twere but for that report, sweetheart, would 'a were thine. Commend a man for his qualities, but take a husband as he is a plain-sufficient, naked man: such a one is for your bed, and such a one is Signor Soranzo, my life for't.

---

mars their standing upright: makes them impotent
wholesome: not diseased

51

Lady Plyant from *The Double Dealer* by William Congreve

First performed in 1693, *The Double Dealer* is a stylish comedy of manners typical of the period, characterised by its elegant wit, epigrammatic dialogue and complicated plot. The action takes place in Lord Touchwood's house on the eve of his niece's wedding.

In brief then: Lady Touchwood is in love with Mellefont, who is about to marry the lovely Cynthia. Maskwell (the double dealer of the title) also loves Cynthia. The out-and-out villain of the piece, he knows Lady Touchwood's secret and, by pretending to love her and be friends with Mellefont, plots to scupper Mellefont's chances with Cynthia and have her for himself. As Cynthia and Mellefont prepare for their wedding celebrations, Lady Touchwood and Maskwell scheme to separate them.

Lady Plyant is a silly, vain, garrulous, credulous woman, easily flattered by male attention. She is second wife to Cynthia's father, Sir Paul Plyant. Lady Touchwood has wickedly planted seeds in her head that Mellefont loves her, and has told Sir Paul that Mellefont is only after Cynthia's money and, moreover, that Mellefont is really in love with Lady Plyant. Sir Paul swallows the story hook, line and sinker, and in an absolute fury tells Lady Plyant what he knows, stoking a fire Lady Touchwood has already lit. He marches his distressed niece from the room leaving a perplexed Mellefont alone with Lady Plyant.

In a scene in which both Mellefont and Lady Plyant are at cross-purposes, she makes a big show of being horrified while at the same time being thoroughly flattered by what she misinterprets as Mellefont's amorous intentions. The subtext is writ large – the comedy deriving from the spectacle of a gullible, middle-aged woman flirting coquettishly in an embarrassing display of ardour thinly disguised as outrage. While instructing the unfortunate Mellefont to control his passion she wrestles ineffectually with her own. After all, she wouldn't want him to leave her without a glimmer of hope for his prospects.

Lady Plyant O name it no more! – Bless me how can you talk of Heaven! and have so much wickedness in your heart? Maybe you don't think it a sin. – They say some of you gentlemen don't think it a sin. – Maybe it is no sin to them that don't think so; indeed, if I did not think it a sin – but still my honour, if it were no sin. – But then, to marry my daughter, for the conveniency of frequent opportunities, I'll never consent to that; as sure as can be, I'll break the match. Nay, nay, rise up! come, you shall see my good nature. I know love is powerful, and nobody can help his passion: 'tis not your fault, nor I swear it is not mine. – How can I help it, if I have charms? and how can you help it if you are made a captive? I swear it is pity it should be a fault. – But my honour, – well, but your honour too – but the sin! – well, but the necessity – O Lord, here's somebody coming, I dare not stay. Well, you must consider of your crime; and strive as much as can be against it, – strive, be sure – but don't be melancholic, don't despair. – But never think that I'll grant you anything; O Lord, no. – But be sure you lay aside all thoughts of the marriage: for though I know you don't love Cynthia, only as a blind to your passion for me, yet it will make me jealous. – O Lord, what did I say? jealous! no, no, I can't be jealous, for I must not love you – therefore don't hope, – but don't despair neither. – O, they're coming! I must fly.

Angelica from *Love for Love* by William Congreve

This wonderful comedy of manners was first performed in 1695 when Congreve was at the height of his powers.

An extravagant lifestyle in the fruitless pursuit of lovely heiress Angelica has left a young rake, Valentine, stony broke and in bad odour with his father, who has offered to honour his debts – but only if he agrees to forgo his inheritance in favour of his younger brother. What ensues is a masterful plot, rich with social observation and hilarious dialogue that addresses the themes of love, money, hypocrisy, inheritance and the age-old conflict between parent and offspring. Valentine employs a variety of strategies to hang on to his fortune and finally secures the affections of his beloved.

Angelica is a coquettish, clever, witty, self-assured young 'spitfire' with an independent fortune, which gives her considerable social standing. She 'commits to no man, and feigns indifference to all'. In this scene she addresses her uncle, Foresight – 'an illiterate old fellow, peevish and positive, superstitious, and pretending to understand astrology, palmistry, physiognomy, omens, dreams' etc. She wants to borrow his coach to go out on the town. When he refuses to lend it she exerts pressure on him by taunting him with the suggestion that his wife is cuckolding him while abroad and mocking his pretentious posturings. The silly old fool is an easy target and the more apoplectic he gets, the more Angelica goads him – her invective growing more ruthless and creative as he rises to the bait. Finally, she heartlessly drags her cousin's old nurse into her colourful inventions, threatening to accuse her of engaging in witchcraft and satanic rites in her uncle's closet until the horrified servant bursts into tears.

When Foresight thinks Angelica knows something about his wife's infidelity, he promises to forgive her and lend the carriage, but they are interrupted by the entrance of a servant and the wicked girl exits with her nose in the air to call a sedan, leaving him hopping with anxiety.

Angelica Uncle, pray lend me your coach, mine's out of order. I
have a mind to go abroad, and if you won't lend me your coach, I'll
take a hackney, or a chair, and leave you to erect a scheme, and find
who's in conjunction with your wife. Why don't you keep her at
home if you are jealous when she's abroad? You know my aunt is a
little retrograde (as you call it) in her nature. Uncle, I'm afraid you
are not lord of the ascendant, ha, ha, ha . . . Nay, uncle, don't be
angry. If you are, I'll reap up all your false prophecies and
divinations. I'll swear you are a nuisance to the neighbourhood.
What a bustle did you keep against the last invisible eclipse, laying
in provision as 'twere for a siege! What a world of fire and candle,
matches and tinderboxes did you purchase! One would have
thought we were ever after to live underground, or at least making a
voyage to Greenland, to inhabit there all the dark season . . . Will
you lend me your coach, or I'll go on. Nay, I'll declare how you
prophesied popery was coming, only because the butler had mislaid
the Apostle spoons, and thought they were lost. Away went religion
and spoon-meat together. – Indeed, uncle, I'll indite you for a
wizard . . . Yes, I can make oath of your unlawful midnight
practices; you and the old nurse there . . . Yes, I saw you together,
through the key-hole of the closet one night, like Saul and the
Witch of Endor, turning the sieve and shears and pricking your
thumbs to write poor innocent servants' names in blood about a
little nutmeg grater which she had forgot in the candle-cup. Nay, I
know something worse if I could speak of it . . . Look to it, nurse. I
can bring witness that you have a great unnatural teat under your
left arm, and he another, and that you suckle a young devil in the
shape of a tabby cat by turns, I can . . . Goodbye, uncle. Call me a
chair. I'll find out my aunt and tell her she must not come home.

---

turning the sieve and shears: a form of divination using a riddle and shears, popular in
Scotland
unnatural teat: the mark of the Devil

Berinthia from *The Relapse* by Sir John Vanburgh

The Relapse, alternatively titled *Virtue in Danger* (although there is precious little virtue in it), premiered at Drury Lane in 1697 and was the hit of the season. It is a flamboyant Restoration comedy – witty, bawdy, vivacious and elegant – exhibiting a rogue's gallery of fops, rakes and coquettes driven by sex, greed and social status.

The primary plot centres on the attempts of the feisty, calculating, smoothly hypocritical and utterly amoral young widow, Berinthia, and her former lover, the womanising Worthy, to get her innocent cousin Amanda into bed with Worthy. Thus leaving the field clear for Berinthia to enjoy her relationship with Amanda's husband, the appropriately named Loveless. While affecting 'sisterly' concern for Amanda, Berinthia sets out with Worthy to convince her that Loveless has a mistress – as indeed he has! But Amanda's dogged determination to trust Loveless and keep her marriage vows intact is proving a fly in the ointment. Worthy believes these can only be 'breached' if she is persuaded of Loveless's infidelity. Berinthia's manipulative skills are enlisted and she comes up with this 'brainwave' to convince Amanda, once and for all.

Here she outlines her plan with anticipatory relish. Amanda is to be lured to Whitehall to 'catch' Loveless with a masked Berinthia. When the betrayal is discovered, Amanda will be in emotional disarray, the unscrupulous Worthy will swoop in to pick up the pieces and Berinthia will have Loveless for herself. Look at the language – 'spring a mine', 'blow her up'. She knows she is playing with fire, but that is half the excitement. Look how the language waxes more colourful as she dramatises Amanda's reaction and Worthy's imagined conquest. By the end, the picture has become so vivid she has almost begun to feel sorry for 'poor Amanda' – if only she were capable of such an emotion.

But Berinthia is thwarted and virtue triumphs when Amanda remains faithful in spite of Worthy's insistent advances, transforming his lust to instant adoration.

Berinthia What think you of springing a mine? I have a thought just now come into my head, how to blow her up at once . . . Faith, I'll do't; and thus the execution of it shall be. We are all invited to my Lord Foppington's tonight to supper; he's come to town with his bride, and makes a ball, with an entertainment of music. Now, you must know, my undoer here, Loveless, says he must needs meet me about some private business (I don't know what 'tis) before we go to the company. To which end he has told his wife one lie, and I have told her another. But to make her amends, I'll go immediately, and tell her a solemn truth. I'll tell her that to my certain knowledge her husband has a rendezvous with his mistress this afternoon; and that if she'll give me her word she'll be satisfied with the discovery, without making any violent inquiry after the woman, I'll direct her to a place where she shall see 'em meet. Now, friend, this I fancy may help you to a critical minute. For home she must go again to dress. You (with your good breeding) come to wait upon us to the ball, find her all alone, her spirit inflamed against her husband for his treason, and her flesh in a heat from some contemplations upon the treachery, her blood on a fire, her conscience in ice; a lover to draw, and the devil to drive. – Ah, poor Amanda!

Lady Wishfort from *The Way of the World* by William Congreve

Congreve wrote this, his last play, in 1700. It is a rollicking, convoluted comedy – a tangle of romantic intrigue, deception, stratagems, posturings, revelations and town and country rivalries. The main plot centres around Mirabell, a typical Restoration beau, and his schemes to marry his beloved Millament, the coquettish ward of ageing Lady Wishfort, who holds her fortune in trust, only to be released if Millament marries a suitor of her choice. Lady Wishfort disapproves of the match, in fact detests Mirabell for thwarting her own delusional advances, so he contrives a plan that hinges on convincing Lady Wishfort to marry 'Sir Rowland', Mirabell's rich uncle (actually Mirabell's trusty servant Waitwell), and then using the threatened scandal to force her hand.

Foible, Lady Wishfort's duplicitous maid, has just been married to Waitwell as part of Mirabell's plan. One of Mirabell's rejected mistresses, who has her own axe to grind, has just spotted Foible talking with 'the enemy' in the park and has reported back to Lady Wishfort. Lady Wishfort challenges Foible who quickly invents a story to cover her back. She goes for the jugular, inventing a catalogue of insults, supposedly voiced by Mirabell, about Lady Wishfort's age and stupidity. Outraged and egged on by Foible, she determines to marry Sir Rowland the following day so that his feckless nephew will be disinherited.

Lady Wishfort is preening, gullible, vainglorious, snobbish and 'wages an unequal battle with time'. The temptation might be to play her as a shrieking harridan, but here she cuts a rather sad, fretful figure as she tries to restore her cracking cosmetic façade and juggles her desire to maintain proper decorum with her desperation to impress. Try to avoid caricature. The comedy comes from her foolish affectations and incongruous self-delusion. The language supplies the broad brush. All Congreve's characters have names apt to their characters, hence Wishfort – wishing for – and what Lady Wishfort wishes for is to be young again and to be loved by a man.

Lady Wishfort   Frippery! superannuated frippery! I'll frippery the villain; I'll reduce him to frippery and rags: a tatterdemallion – I hope to see him hung with tatters, like a Long-Lane penthouse, or a gibbet-thief. A slander-mouthed railer: I warrant the spendthrift prodigal's in debt as much as the million lottery, or the whole court upon a birthday. I'll spoil his credit with his tailor. Yes, he shall have my niece with her fortune, he shall. He has put me out of all patience. I shall never recompose my features, to receive Sir Rowland with any economy of face. This wretch has fretted me that I am absolutely decayed. Look, Foible . . . Let me see the glass – cracks, sayest thou? Why I am arrantly flayed – I look like an old peeled wall. Thou must repair me, Foible, before Sir Rowland comes; or I shall never keep up to my picture . . . But art thou sure Sir Rowland will not fail to come? Or will a' not fail when he does come? Will he be importunate, Foible, and push? For if he should not be importunate – I shall never break decorums – I shall die with confusion, if I am forced to advance. – Oh no, I can never advance – I shall swoon if he should expect advances. No, I hope Sir Rowland is better bred, than to put a lady to the necessity of breaking her forms. I won't be too coy neither. – I won't give him despair – but a little disdain is not amiss; a little scorn is alluring . . . Yes, but tenderness becomes me best – A sort of dyingness. – You see that picture has a sort of a – ha Foible? A swimmingness in the eyes. – Yes, I'll look so. – My niece affects it; but she wants features. Is Sir Rowland handsome? Let my toilet be removed – I'll dress above. I'll receive Sir Rowland here. Is he handsome? Don't answer me. I won't know: I'll be surprised. I'll be taken by surprise.

Mrs Sullen from *The Beaux' Stratagem* by George Farquhar

The Beaux' Stratagem was Farquhar's last comedy. He died not long after its first performance in 1707.

A 'situation' comedy of manners in which everyone has a stratagem for escape from his or her circumstances, the basic plot is very simple. Two fashionable gentlemen, Aimwell and Archer, leave London for Lichfield in search of wealthy marriages, a strategem to salvage their ruined fortunes. They arrive an inn, posing as a noble lord and his servant. They quickly set their sights on Dorinda, a beautiful young heiress, and Mrs Sullen who is unhappily married to Dorinda's doltish brother. Tension rises as Archer sets his cap at Mrs Sullen and she is more and more drawn towards adultery.

An attractive youngish woman trapped in a loveless marriage with a country blockhead, Mrs Sullen loathes country life and longs for the fashionable city. She is chained to her husband by financial dependence, is physically and emotionally starved of affection and feels she has been 'cheated into slavery, mocked by a promise of comfortable society into a wilderness of solitude'.

Here she is complaining to her sister-in-law about her life. Dorinda asks why, if it is so abhorrent, have poets and philosophers found so much pleasure in the countryside but Mrs Sullen is unconvinced. The only rich poet or philosopher is a dead one, she says, and none of the pastoral lovers in their verses are foolish enough to marry.

As she shares her discontent, the aptly named Squire Sullen approaches. The uncomplimentary picture she paints of his behaviour and their relationship is colourful and wonderfully graphic. He is a bonehead. He doesn't talk to her. He comes home drunk, falls over furniture and disturbs her sleep. She is certainly 'rattling her marital chains' and there is serious point at the heart of her tale about what married women are forced to tolerate in eighteenth-century England without remedy or escape.

Mrs Sullen   Did you ever see a poet or philosopher worth ten thousand pound? If you can show me such a man, I'll lay you fifty pound you'll find him somewhere within the weekly bills. Not that I disapprove rural pleasures, as the poets have painted them; in their landscape, every Phyllis has her Corydon, every murmuring stream, and every flowery mead, gives fresh alarms to love. Besides, you'll find that their couples were never married. – But yonder I see my Corydon, and a sweet swain it is, Heaven knows! Come, Dorinda, don't be angry; he's my husband, and your brother: and, between both, is he not a sad brute? O sister, sister! if ever you marry, beware of a sullen, silent sot, one that's always musing, but never thinks. There's some diversion in a talking blockhead; and since a woman must wear chains, I would have the pleasure of hearing 'em rattle a little. Now you shall see, but take this by the way: – He came home this morning at his usual hour of four, wakened me out of a sweet dream of something else, by tumbling over the tea-table, which he broke all to pieces; after his man and he had rolled about the room like sick passengers in a storm, he comes flounce into bed, dead as a salmon into a fishmonger's basket; his feet cold as ice, his breath hot as a furnace, and his hands and his face as greasy as his flannel nightcap. – O, matrimony! – He tosses up the clothes with a barbarous swing over his shoulders, disorders the whole economy of my bed, leaves me half naked, and my whole night's comfort is the tuneable serenade of that wakeful nightingale, his nose! O the pleasure of counting the melancholy clock by a snoring husband! But now, sister, you shall see how handsomely, being a well-bred man, he will beg my pardon.

---

the weekly bills: The London bills of mortality were early-eighteenth-century newspaper reports of diseases and deaths during the week
Phyllis and Corydon: a shepherdess and shepherd from pastoral poetry
swain: a lover in pastoral poetry, although it also means farm labourer, fitting Mrs Sullen's poor opinion of the Squire
since a woman must wear chains: Mrs Sullen's realistic assessment of the role of women in eighteenth-century marriage

Julia from *The Rivals* by Richard Brinsley Sheridan

One of the most hilarious of late-Restoration comedies, *The Rivals* was first performed in 1775. Set in Bath, a fashionable resort for the aspiring middle classes and aristocracy of eighteenth-century England, it is a skilful social satire that snipes at love, marriage, class and wealth.

Fed on a diet of romantic fiction, young and beautiful Lydia Languish concludes that the only way to ensure true love is to eschew her riches and marry a poor man. To win her hand, dashing Captain Jack Absolute, wealthy son of a baronet, Sir Anthony, poses as Ensign Beverley – the impecunious lover of her fantasies. Meanwhile, Sir Anthony is trying to arrange Jack's marriage to Lydia through her guardian, the language-mangling Mrs Malaprop, and in consequence, Jack becomes a rival to himself.

Simultaneously, Jack's best friend, Faulkland, has fallen in love with Sir Anthony's ward, Julia. Although his love is returned, Faulkland is consumed with jealousy and doubt, driving him to submit the constant, self-possessed and steadfast Julia to numerous validations of her love. Julia has tolerated this with some distress, attributing his behaviour to an excess of humility and lack of self-worth.

Here, Faulkland confides to Julia that he has been drawn into a dangerous quarrel and must leave the country. She responds by offering to give up everything and go with him, and Faulkland has to admit it is yet another story. Although he promises she has finally proved her love, it is a test too far for Julia. She has run out of patience with his constant suspicion and gives him his marching orders.

Although Julia's dignified suffering should be played truthfully, the comedy derives from Sheridan's parody of a noble, self-sacrificing heroine as Julia couches her feelings in the ridiculously overblown language of high romance (inspired no doubt by her reading matter) which she plays to the hilt.

Julia Hold, Faulkland! – that you are free from a crime, which I before feared to name, Heaven knows how sincerely I rejoice! – These are tears of thankfulness for that! But that your cruel doubts should have urged you to an imposition that has wrung my heart, gives me now a pang more keen than I can express! Yet hear me. – My father loved you, Faulkland! and you preserved the life that tender parent gave me; in his presence I pledged my hand – joyfully pledged it – where before I had given my heart. When, soon after, I lost that parent, it seemed to me that Providence had, in Faulkland, shown me whither to transfer, without a pause, my grateful duty as well as my affection: hence I have been content to bear from you what pride and delicacy would have forbid me from another. – I will not upbraid you by repeating how you have trifled with my sincerity. – After such a year of trial, I might have flattered myself that I should not have been insulted with a new probation of my sincerity, as cruel as unnecessary! I now see it is not in your nature to be content or confident in love. With this conviction – I never will be yours. While I had hopes that my persevering attention and unreproaching kindness might in time reform your temper, I should have been happy to have gained a dearer influence over you; but I will not furnish you with a licensed power to keep alive an incorrigible fault at the expense of one who never would contend with you. But one word more. – As my faith has once been given you, I never will barter it with another. – I shall pray for your happiness with the truest sincerity; and the dearest blessing I can ask of Heaven to send you will be to charm you from that unhappy temper, which alone has prevented the performance of our solemn engagement. – All I request of *you* is, that you will yourself reflect upon this infirmity, and when you number up the many true delights it has deprived you of – let it not be your *least* regret that it lost you the love of one – who would have followed you in beggary through the world!

Helen from *The Family Legend* by Joanna Baillie

The Scottish playwright Joanna Baillie (1762–1851) was admired by Byron and was the protégée of Sir Walter Scott. *The Family Legend* was one of her most successful plays and received a celebrated production at Drury Lane in 1821.

Two rival clans, the Argylls and the Macleans, are united by a politically expedient marriage, when Helen, the Earl of Argyll's daughter, becomes the wife of Maclean, sacrificing her love for Sir Hubert de Grey by doing so. The bond is cemented when a son is born. But hostilities are renewed when Benlora, the fiercest of the Macleans, is released from captivity and sees the peace as an affront. Benlora and other Maclean nobles devise a plot to murder Helen and reignite the conflict. Promising Maclean that they 'will not spill Helen's blood', they leave her on a rock to drown, but de Grey rescues her and she returns to her father's castle. Her brother and de Grey press for vengeance but the Earl counsels caution, fearful for his grandson whom Helen has left behind on the Island of Mull.

Thinking Helen is dead, Maclean sends word of his impending visit to the Earl to offer his condolences. De Grey secretly intends to use the opportunity of this distraction to rescue Helen's son. In this scene he comes to Helen's apartment in the castle – she thinks to say a final honourable goodbye. Both are feeling distressed and miserable.

Helen is a young noble woman who bears her vicissitudes with character and fortitude. Because she loves de Grey, she is doing all she can to make him feel better about leaving by accepting her fate with optimism and good heart, telling him that although they must be parted, they will always have news of each other, and he can think of her at peace in her father's house. This is a speech of tender farewell spoken with simplicity and love.

The Family Legend is written in iambic pentameter. Each line has its own energy and will carry Helen's heartfelt emotion and intentions if you trust its measure.

Helen

O go not from me with that mournful look!
Alas! thy generous heart, depressed and sunk,
Looks on my state too sadly. –
I am not, as thou thinkst, a thing so lost
In woe and wretchedness. – Believe not so!
All whom misfortune with her rudest blasts
Hath buffeted, to gloomy wretchedness
Are not therefore abandoned. Many souls
From cloistered cells, from hermits' caves, from holds
Of lonely banishment, and from the dark
And dreary prison-house, do raise their thoughts
With humble cheerfulness to heaven, and feel
A hallowed quiet, almost akin to joy;
And may not I, by heaven's kind mercy aided,
Weak as I am, with some good courage bear
What is appointed for me? – O be cheered!
And let not sad and mournful thoughts of me
Depress thee thus. – When thou art far away,
Thou'lt hear, the while, that in my father's house
I spend my peaceful days, and let it cheer thee.
I too shall every southern stranger question,
Whom chance may to these regions bring, and learn
Thy fame and prosperous state.

Mencía from *The Surgeon of Honour* by Calderón de la Barca (translated by Gwynne Edwards)

Calderón is one of the great playwrights of the Golden Age of Spanish drama. This play, written in 1635, is a disturbing baroque horror story about codes of honour carried to tragic extremes – a motif that figures in several of Calderón's plays. The chief protagonist is the Spanish nobleman Don Gutierre Alfonso Solis, a man obsessed with preserving his honour at any cost. Believing that his beloved, Donna Leonor, has been unfaithful, Don Gutierre abandons her and marries the beautiful young noblewoman Donna Mencía instead, not realising that the King's brother, Don Enrique, previously wooed her.

At the beginning of the play Don Enrique is injured in a fall from his horse and carried by chance to the couple's house. Unconscious, he is put to bed while his friend Don Arias – unaware of Donna Mencía's marriage – tells her that Don Enrique's love is greater than ever.

Donna Mencía is left alone to wrestle with the conflicting emotions that Don Arias's words and Don Enrique's unexpected arrival have had on her. She is on an emotional rack. This speech is the articulation of an anguished internal dialogue. She is desperate to be able to express her love for Enrique which honour forbids her to acknowledge. She is married to a man she does not love and trapped by the tyrannical code of conduct of the times. Even thinking such tender thoughts is dishonourable. She tries to dismiss them, tries to convince herself that self-denial is the one true test of virtue. Poor woman. It is the only course open to her.

At the end of the speech Don Enrique comes round and the lovers find themselves face to face.

The speech is written in lines of eight syllables, with irregular rhythms and internal rhymes – a structure the translator has chosen to 'achieve some of the liveliness and musicality of Calderón's original'. Pay careful attention to the punctuation and give the verse space to breathe and you will find its emotional measure.

Mencía

Now they are gone,
I am alone. If only I,
With honour's kind consent, could give
Free reign to my true sentiment.
If only I could voice my feelings,
Shattering the icy silence of
This prison where my passion lies
In chains, its flames but ashes, while
The dying of its embers tells
Me to remember: 'Here was love!'
But what am I now saying? What
Am I now doing, knowing who I am?
The wind must now return to me
The words it's borne away, before,
Though seeming to be lost, they say
To someone else those secret things
That never must be spoken by myself.
For if by general consent,
It is agreed I have no right
To my own feelings, I must take
My sole delight in now denying them.
Is not the only honest virtue
Virtue tested? Gold is perfected in
The crucible, the magnet tested
By iron, diamond by diamond,
Base metal in the hottest fire.
So must my self-denial be
The only test of honour's worth.
I pray to heaven, take pity on
Me now. If I must live, as I
Now die in silence, let it be!
Enrique! My lord!

Agnès from *The School for Wives* by Molière (translated by Richard Wilbur)

This lively satirical comedy was first performed at Palais-Royal in 1662, with Molière himself playing the central character – wealthy, middle-aged roué, Monsieur Arnolphe.

Arnolphe, who has long resisted marriage, returns home after a short absence to announce his intention to marry Agnès, his obedient little ward whom he has raised from infancy to be ignorant of the wicked ways of the world. He has it all worked out. Marriage to such a sweet, dependent girl will be his guarantee against being cuckolded.

But when Horace, the son of an old friend, comes to visit, he confides in Arnolphe that he has fallen in love with a beautiful young woman who is kept a virtual prisoner by her jealous guardian, an 'aristocrat' called Monsieur de la Souche – not realising this is a name the arrogant Arnolphe has recently adopted. Arnolphe listens with alarm as Horace waxes lyrical about Agnès, telling him how she has responded to his overtures and of his intention to steal her away. Perhaps Agnès is not as innocent as she seems?

In this scene Arnolphe has called Agnès out under the pretext of a morning stroll, to establish how far things have gone between them. Horace's declaration of love and amorous attentions have left Agnès in raptures. She is a convent-educated, naive, artless young woman with no inkling of Arnolphe's plans for her future. Unaware of having done anything wrong, she ingenuously tells her guardian of her meeting with Horace. She is so consumed by the 'first, fine careless rapture' of young love, and so absorbed by Horace and the story of their first meeting that she is scarcely aware of her guardian's growing agitation. Perhaps she is just beginning to appreciate the effect she has on men? Innocent she might be, but ignorant she is not, and under the influence of love, she quickly grows up.

This translation, like Molière's original, is in rhyming couplets, which can be a problem for actors. The challenge is to make them sound like 'real talk'. Be led by the punctuation, the meaning and the character naivety, rather than the line endings, otherwise the dialogue will sound sing-song and stilted.

Agnès

I disobeyed you, but when I tell you why,
You'll say that you'd have done the same as I.

[**Arnolphe**

Perhaps; well, tell me how this thing occurred.

Agnès

It's the most amazing story you ever heard.]

I was sewing, out on the balcony, in the breeze,
When I noticed someone strolling under the trees.
It was a fine young man, who caught my eye
And made me a deep bow as he went by.
I, not to be convicted of a lack
Of manners, very quickly nodded back.
At once, the young man bowed to me again.
I bowed to him a second time, and then
It wasn't very long until he made
A third deep bow, which I of course repaid.
He left, but kept returning, and as he passed,
He'd bow, each time, more gracefully than the last,
While I, observing as he came and went,
Gave each new bow a fresh acknowledgment.
Indeed, had night not fallen, I declare
I think that I might still be sitting there,
And bowing back each time he bowed to me,
For fear he'd think me less polite than he.

[**Arnolphe**

Go on.]

Agnès

Then an old woman came, next day,
And found me standing in the entryway.
She said to me, 'May Heaven bless you, dear,
And keep you beautiful for many a year.
God, who bestowed on you such grace and charm,
Did not intend those gifts to do men harm,

And you should know that there's a heart which bears
A wound which you've inflicted unawares.'

[Arnolphe (*aside*)

Old witch! Old tool of Satan! Damn her hide!]

Agnès

'You say I've wounded somebody?' I cried.
'Indeed you have,' she said. 'The victim's he
Whom yesterday saw you from the balcony.'
'But how could such a thing occur?' I said;
'Can I have dropped some object on his head?'
'No,' she replied, 'your bright eyes dealt the blow;
Their glances are the cause of all his woe.'
'Good heavens, Madam,' said I in great surprise,
'Is there some dread contagion in my eyes?'
'Ah, yes, my child,' said she. 'Your eyes dispense,
Unwittingly, a fatal influence:
The poor young man has dwindled to a shade;
And if you cruelly deny him aid,
I greatly fear,' the kind old woman went on,
'That two days more will see him dead and gone.'
'Heavens,' I answered, 'that would be sad indeed.
But what can I do for him? What help does he need?'
'My child,' said she, 'he only asks of you
The privilege of a little interview;
It is your eyes alone which now can save him,
And cure him of the malady they gave him.'
'If that's the case,' I said, 'I can't refuse;
I'll gladly see him, whenever he may choose.'

[Arnolphe (*aside*)

O 'kind old woman'! O vicious sorceress!
May Hell reward you for your cleverness!]

Agnès

And so I saw him, which brought about his cure.
You'll grant I did the proper thing, I'm sure.

How could I have the conscience to deny
The succour he required, and let him die –
I, who so pity anyone in pain,
And cannot bear to see a chicken slain?

[**Arnolphe** (*aside*)

It's clear that she has meant no wrong, and I

Must blame that foolish trip I took, whereby

I left her unprotected from the lies

That rascally seducers can devise.

Oh, what if that young wretch, with one bold stroke,

Has compromised her? That would be no joke.]

Agnès

What's wrong? You seem a trifle irritated
Was there some harm in what I just related?

Elmire from *Tartuffe* by Molière (translated by Christopher Hampton)

Written in 1664, this is a comic satire on religious bigotry, vanity, hypocrisy and greed set in seventeenth-century Catholic France. Tartuffe, posing as a religious zealot, has wormed his way into the affections of wealthy, autocratic nobleman, Organ, who has installed him in his household in order to exercise control over his family and offer an example of piety.

Tartuffe's bogus religious fervour is laid on with a trowel and he has convinced the gullible Orgon he offers 'a gateway to heaven'. Orgon is completely taken in – although it is clear to everyone else that Tartuffe is a bigoted sanctimonious fraud, after Orgon's money.

When Orgon determines to marry off his horrified daughter Mariane to Tartuffe, in spite of her love for Valère, the whole family is up in arms. Mariane's stepmother, Elmire, seeks out Tartuffe to beg him to refuse Mariane, but he responds by trying to seduce her. Orgon's son, Damis, overhears their exchanges and tells his father of the treachery, but Orgon is so besotted with Tartuffe, he takes his side and banishes Damis from the house.

Elmire, a wise and virtuous woman in her middle years, sees right through Tartuffe's posturing. Realising that reasoning with Orgon is useless, she decides something must be done to save him from his own folly and takes matters into her own hands. She asks Tartuffe to meet her and persuades Orgon (who can't believe anything bad of Tartuffe) to hide under a table so he can witness Tartuffe's advances for himself.

Creating an air of secrecy and intimacy, Elmire sets the scene. She plays Tartuffe at his own game, appealing to him on every level as she pretends to be a weak and modest female, overcome by a passion she is unable to contain. Surely he must know that when a woman says 'no', she really means 'yes' – that she has been playing 'hard to get' because she is so smitten? Her behaviour is presented as a paradox which makes perfect sense.

Shrewd and clever, Elmire knows exactly which buttons

to press to flush Tartuffe into the open. Remember, she has
an audience. She is putting her virtue on the line for her
husband's sake.

_____

Elmire

> Yes, there's a secret I must tell you. But,
> before I do, would you please close the door,
> and make sure no one's likely to surprise us.

[**Tartuffe** *goes to close the door and comes back*.]

Elmire

> We don't want a repeat of what just happened
> for anything, I've never been so shocked.
> Damis gave me a dreadful fright, on your
> behalf, and, as you saw, I did my best
> to calm him down and frustrate his intentions.
> It's true I was so worried that it never
> occurred to me to contradict his story;
> but, thank God, for that very reason things
> turned out much better and less dangerously.
> Your reputation soon dispelled the storm,
> my husband couldn't think badly of you;
> and to show his contempt for crude suspicions,
> he wants us to spend lots of time together;
> and that's why I can be alone with you
> here, without any fear of being judged,
> and what allows me to reveal to you
> what I should perhaps keep back a little longer:
> that I'm prepared to entertain your suit.

[**Tartuffe**

> I'm not quite sure I follow you, Madame,
> just now you gave a very different answer.]

Elmire

> Oh, well, if my refusal put you off,
> you must know very little about women!
> You're no good at interpreting what's meant
> by such an obviously weak defence.
> On these occasions modesty is bound
> to be in conflict with our tender feelings.

However right yielding to love may feel,
it's always slightly shaming to admit it.
At first we fight against it; but the way
we do so is a sign of our surrender;
our voice, for virtue's sake, protesting feebly
against our instincts, gives the kind of no
which promises you everything. Well, now,
I suppose that's a pretty damning confession,
I haven't paid much heed to modesty;
but, since it's in the open now at last,
would I have tried so hard to silence Damis?
I ask you, would I have so quietly listened
to that long declaration of your love?
Would I have taken it the way I did
unless something about it gave me pleasure?
And when I tried to blackmail you myself
not to accept this newly arranged wedding,
what did my urgency suggest to you,
if not that you now meant a lot to me,
and that this proposed marriage would upset me,
by, at the very least, making me share
a love I wanted for myself alone?

Frosine from *The Miser* by Molière
(translated by John Wood)

The Miser was first performed in 1668 but was so ill-received it closed after only four performances. It has subsequently become one of Molière's most popular comedies and Harpagon, the tight-fisted sexagenarian of the title, one of his most notorious characters.

Harpagon, whose every action is dictated by greed, decides his children are costing him too much money, so he plans to marry them off to suitors who will relieve him of financial responsibility – an old man who won't demand a dowry for his daughter, and a rich widow for his son. Unfortunately, both are in love with other people and have rather different ideas. The matter is complicated further because his son is in love with the beautiful, but penniless Marianne whom Harpagon has decided to marry himself.

In this scene Harpagon has enlisted the aid of the matchmaker Frosine to help him woo the youthful Marianne. Frosine is something of an independent businesswoman who lives on her wits – a wheeler-dealer who makes her way in the world by acting as a go-between and making herself useful wherever her scheming services might be required. She prides herself in knowing all the strategies to charm and flatter men, 'stroke them the right way, arouse their sympathy and find their soft spots'. This is what she is up to here.

In this speech she uses her wiles to promise Harpagon satisfaction, sycophantically playing on Harpagon's scrimping nature. Notice there is nothing sentimental, no reference to love here. This is entirely a business transaction from both their points of view. She is a practised saleswoman, describing the advantages of her product (Marianne) with a good knowledge of her market. She speaks of 'considerations', what Marianne will 'bring in', evaluating her frugal nature and simple tastes in terms of monetary advantage – totting up the sums on her mental calculator, a tactic she knows will appeal. She uses all her cunning to set the old miser's mind at rest about the 'hidden' financial benefits of the match – all the expenses Marianne *won't* incur – and not without a shrewd eye to prising open Harpagon's tight purse strings for herself.

She usually gets what she wants out of her clients, but Harpagon will prove a tough nut to crack.

_____

Frosine Did you ever know me start a job and not finish it? I really have a wonderful talent for matchmaking. There's nobody I couldn't pair off, given a little time to arrange things. I really think, if I took it into my head, I could match the Grand Turk and the Venetian Republic! Not that there was anything very difficult about this little business of yours. I am friendly with the two ladies and have talked to them both about you and told the mother of the intentions you have formed in regard to Marianne from seeing her pass along the street and taking the air at her window.

[**Harpagon** And her reply?

Frosine She was delighted by the proposal, and when I intimated that you would like her daughter to be present this evening at the signing of your own daughter's marriage contract she agreed without hesitation and put her in my charge.

Harpagon You see, I am committed to giving a supper for Seigneur Anselme, Frosine, and I shall be very pleased if she will join the party too.

Frosine Good. She is to visit your daughter after dinner and then go to the fair, which she wants to do, and return in time for supper.

Harpagon Very well. I will lend them my carriage and they can go down together.

Frosine That's the very thing for her!

Harpagon Now, have you sounded the mother as to what dowry she can give her daughter, Frosine? Have you told her she must make an effort to contribute something and put herself to some pinching and scraping on an occasion like this? After all, nobody is going to marry a girl unless she brings something with her.]

Frosine Why, this girl will bring you twelve thousand a year.

[**Harpagon** Twelve thousand a year!

Frosine Yes.]

In the first place she's been brought up on a very spare diet. She is a girl who is used to living on salad and milk, apples and cheese, so she'll need no elaborate table, none of your rich broths or eternal barley concoctions, nor any of the delicacies other women would require, and that's no small consideration. It might well amount to three thousand francs a year at least. Moreover, her tastes are simple; she has not any hankering after extravagant dresses, expensive jewellery, or sumptuous furnishings which young women of her age are so fond of – and this item alone means more than four thousand a year. Then, again, she has a very strong objection to playing for money, a most unusual thing in a woman nowadays. I know one woman in our neighbourhood who has lost twenty thousand francs at cards this year. Suppose we reckon only a quarter of that – five thousand a year for cards and four thousand on clothes and jewellery, that's nine thousand, and another three thousand on food – that gives you your twelve thousand a year, doesn't it?

[**Harpagon** Yes, it's not that bad, but all these calculations don't amount to anything tangible.

Frosine Come, come!]

Do you mean to say that a modest appetite, a sober taste in dress, and a dislike of card playing don't amount to anything tangible? Why, they are a marriage portion and an inheritance rolled into one!]

Albina from *Britannicus* by Jean Racine (translated by Robert David MacDonald)

Written in 1669, *Britannicus* is set during the last days of the Roman Empire in the palace of Rome's tyrannical young Emperor, Nero. It explores themes of political intrigue, corruption and the abuse of power, and is fuelled by the unhealthy relationship between Agrippina and her son Nero, who owes his throne to his mother's murderous strategies to dispossess his stepbrother, Britannicus, the rightful heir. It charts how Agrippina loses her position in the court as Nero turns against her in his pursuit of absolute power and his machinations to take Junia, Britannicus' lover, from him.

This speech comes right at the end of the play. Nero has poisoned Britannicus, his rival to the throne as well as in love. When she hears the news, Junia runs from the palace, consumed by grief, and seeks refuge with the Vestal Virgins.

All the action takes place offstage and Albina, a kindly middle-aged noblewoman, confidante to Agrippina, is telling the story. She describes Junia's desperate flight and Nero's distraught ravings when he discovers Junia is beyond his reach. In Albina's eyewitness account, with the horror and tragedy of events still fresh in her mind, she plugs us into the emotion of each of the characters as the story unfolds. Moreover, she fears for Nero's sanity and safety and is trying to impress on his mother the urgency of the situation. But Agrippina, appalled by Nero's monstrous nature, is unmoved.

Britannicus is written in rhyming couplets. Within the vagaries of the English language, the translator has largely stuck to Racine's twelve-syllable meter. Pay close attention to the rhyme, punctuation and line endings. These are valuable guides to character, pacing and shifts in thought process. Consider, for instance, the dash before '– where Nero cannot follow'. Or the quotation marks around Junia's direct speech. (She wants to make the most of her story perhaps?) Or the full stop after 'Drenching Junia.' (A pause for dramatic effect?) Go through the speech line by line to create each image as the story unfolds.

Albina

The Emperor is condemned to an unending sorrow.
She is not dead, she is – where Nero may not follow.
When she escaped from here, she ran as if to go
To see Octavia, but then she took a road
That leads to nowhere. I watched her as she ran, distraught,
Out of the palace gates. She soon found what she sought,
The statue of Augustus. Falling down, she wept
At the marble feet, her arms around him, prayed: 'Accept
My prayers, Prince; by this cold stone that I embrace,
Protect, both now and henceforth, the last of all your race.
Rome has just seen the murder of the only one
Of all of us who worthily could have called himself your son.
They wished me to betray him after he had died.
But I must keep faith with him. So I here decide
To dedicate myself to that eternal god,
Whose altar you now share, your virtue's just reward.'
Meanwhile the people, by the confusion worse confounded,
Press on her from all sides, until she is surrounded
By a multitude, that, moved by her tears, and pitying
Her obvious distress, take her beneath their wing,
And lead her to the temple, where they still maintain,
As in ages past, the eternal Vestal flame.
Nero sees all of this, but does not dare to enter:
Narcissus, more intent to please, makes for the centre,
Approaching Junia, fearlessly, with utter lack
Of shame, begins, profanely, to try to force her back –
A blasphemy that falls victim to a hundred blows:
His sacrilegious blood incontinently flows,
Drenching Junia. Nero, barely comprehending
What he is looking at, abandons him to his bloody ending –
And goes back. All avoid him. Silent, grim,
Junia's name the only sound that comes from him.

Lisette from *Careless Vows* by Pierre Marivaux (translated by John Walters)

First performed in 1732, this comedy about the sexual politics of love was booed on its first night and only ran for nine performances. Yet it was Marivaux's favourite and its witty exploration of the psychology of relationships feels very contemporary.

Their fathers have arranged a marriage between Lucile and Damis, but both share an aversion to the married state. Nevertheless, they agree to a meeting to keep them happy. But in fact Lisette, Lucile's maid, goes instead of her mistress while Lucile hides to overhear the conversation. When she learns Damis shares her antipathy to marriage she reveals herself to declare her own. Lisette encourages the couple to solemnly vow they will never belong to one another. The self-interested Lisette knows if her mistress marries she will lose all her authority in the household. Unfortunately for her, Damis is captivated by Lucile's beauty at first sight and Lucile is similarly smitten.

The comedy of the play hinges on the reluctance of the lovers to make the first move and declare their love, and the machinations of their canny servants to manipulate the situation to their own advantage.

Lisette is a bright, impertinent, machinating forthright and feisty young woman who is in love with Damis's servant Frontin. As a result of their interventions Lucile's father decides that, as Lucile cannot love Damis, he should marry her sister, Phenice, instead. Afraid she will be sent packing, Lisette and Frontin determine to sort out the mess they have created and bring the intransigent couple together so love can take its natural course. In this scene she has reached the end of her patience with their pussyfooting reticence. She pays no lip-service to the servant/master relationship, berating the couple for their stupid entrenched positions and their toings and froings around their feelings. She seems to know a great deal about sexual politics. She can scarcely contain her frustration as she tries to sting them into sorting things out once and for all.

Lisette Yes, madame, I'm leaving. But before I go, I have to speak. You ask me who I'm getting at. Both of you, madame, both of you! Yes, I would love with all my heart to take away from this gentleman – who has nothing to say and whose silence makes my blood boil – I would love to take away from him his scruples about the ridiculous agreement he has made with you, which I regret having let you make, and which is making you both suffer, one as much as the other. As for you, madame, I don't know how you see these things, but if ever a man had taken a vow never to say 'I love you' to me, oh then I would take a vow to cast the lie in his teeth. He would find out what respect he owed me. I would spare him nothing of all that is most dangerous, shameless, and deadly in the good old flirtatious armoury of looks, words, and glances. That's where I would put my pride, and not in holding myself painfully aloof as you are doing and saying to myself: 'Let's see what he says, let's see what he doesn't say, let him speak, let him begin, it's up to him, it's not up to me, my sex, my pride, the rules of etiquette,' and a thousand other useless ways of dealing with the poor trembling gentleman, who has the goodness to be afraid that his love might alarm and annoy you. Love annoy us! What planet are you from, then? Oh, for heaven's sake, sir, why don't you get annoyed good and proper! Do us that honour! Be brave, attack us! *That* ritual will make your fortune, and you will understand one another. Because up until now there's nothing to be seen in what the two of you are saying. There's 'yes', there's 'no', there's for, there's against, there's going away, there's coming back, there's calling back, there's no way of understanding it. Goodbye, I've finished. I've sorted you out, now take advantage of it. Come on, Frontin.

Mirandolina from *Mirandolina* by Carlo Goldoni (translated by Frederick Davies)

The prolific Goldoni, one of Italy's best-loved playwrights, wrote nearly two hundred plays between 1748 and 1762. *Mirandolina*, written in 1760, is a comedy of great charm and wit and considered one of his masterpieces.

Mirandolina, a young woman of marriageable age, runs an inn in Florence recently inherited from her father. Three noblemen – a Marquis, a Count and a Baron – are in residence. The Count and the Marquis are madly in love with her and furiously jealous of each other. They vie for her affections and while Mirandolina has no time for either of them, she is happy to string them along as long as they pay their bills. The Baron, by contrast, is a rude misogynist who complains about the service and treats Mirandolina like a maid. In fact, he would rather have the plague than a wife!

In this scene the Marquis has just made an inept and blustering marriage proposal leaving Mirandolina alone to scoff at his offer. She is beautiful, earthy, teasing, manipulative, intelligent, unpredictable, independent and self-assured – a natural charmer who knows she can have any man she wants. But she is not ready to settle down with anyone yet – although she has had countless offers – she just wants to have fun. On the other hand, the Baron's misogynist attitudes have put her nose somewhat out of joint. She is used to rather different attentions and determines to use all her womanly wiles to make the Baron fall in love with her. She is equipped for the challenge in every department and relishes the prospect of giving him a run for his money. Actually, she is rather bored with men falling at her feet, so this will spice her life up a bit.

She succeeds, of course, but discovers that she is playing with fire when the Baron proves as overzealous a lover as he was a woman-hater and Mirandolina learns a timely lesson about the nature of love before making an unpredictable choice of husband.

Mirandolina   Huh! Marry him! His Excellency Signor the Marquis Skinflint. That would be the day! The husbands I'd have, if I'd married all that had wanted to marry me! They've only got to enter this Inn and they fall in love with me and think they can marry me on the spot. Except this Signor Baron, the ill-mannered lout! What right's he got to think himself too high and mighty to be civil to me? Nobody else who's ever stopped at this Inn has ever treated me so! I certainly don't expect him to fall in love with me at first sight – but to behave like that! That sort of thing infuriates me. So he hates women? Doesn't want anything to do with them? The poor fool. He hasn't met the woman yet who knows how to set about him. But he will. Oh, yes, he will, all right. And, who knows if he hasn't just met her. Yes, this fellow might be exactly what I need. I'm sick to death of men who run after me. As for marriage – there's plenty of time for that. I want to enjoy my freedom first. And here's a chance to really enjoy it. Yes, I'll use every art I have to conquer this enemy of women!

Marceline from *The Marriage of Figaro* by Beaumarchais (translated by John Wood)

Written in 1781, *The Marriage of Figaro* waited three years for its first performance at the Comédie-Française after Louis XVI banned it, declaring it should never be performed. Lampooning the French class system in its portrayal of a lecherous, incompetent aristocrat outwitted by a crafty manservant, it foreshadowed the French Revolution of 1789.

Its convoluted plot takes place in Count Almaviva's castle near Seville (the content too sensitive to set in France). It focuses on the Count's designs to exercise his 'droit de seigneur' (the right of the feudal lord to sleep with the brides of his servants on the wedding night) over his wife's feisty maid, Suzanne, who is just about to marry his valet, Figaro. While Figaro and Suzanne plot to thwart him, Marceline, the middle-aged castle housekeeper and constant companion to Bartholo, plots to scupper their wedding so Marceline can have Figaro herself. Figaro has signed a contract promising to marry Marceline if he is unable to repay a loan.

In this scene a court has been set up in the castle where Marceline is pressing her claim, as Figaro has no money to settle his debt. The court finds in Marceline's favour, but Figaro argues that he is a foundling and can't marry without the permission of his parents, from whom he was stolen by gypsies as a baby. He proves his 'noble' parentage by revealing the 'family crest' – a spatula tattooed on his arm. Marceline recognises it immediately and to general astonishment reveals herself as Figaro's mother and names Bartholo as the father who had promised to marry her if their child was found. Figaro is horrified by his lowly parentage and Bartholo tries to wriggle out of his promise, dubbing his newly discovered son 'a deplorable youth', at which Marceline launches into this general indictment of men.

Marceline is described in Beaumarchais' notes as 'a woman of intelligence and of naturally lively temperament but the errors of her youth and subsequent experiences have chastened her'. Here she presents herself as the personification of virtue betrayed, the victim of a seducer – splendid, defiant and warming to her theme. The speech ends on motherly advice to her newfound son to live for the future and enjoy his happiness.

Marceline   Ay! Deplorable! More so than you think! I won't attempt to deny my faults – they have been fully exposed today! But it's hard to have to expiate them after thirty years of decent living. I was by nature good and so remained as long as I was allowed to do so, but just at the age when we are beset by illusions, in experience, and necessity, when seducers besiege us and want stabs us in the back, what can a young girl do against the serried ranks of her enemies? The very man who judges us so severely now has probably compassed the ruin of a dozen such unfortunates himself!

[**Figaro**   Those who are most blameworthy are the least generous themselves. That's always the way!]

Marceline   You men, lost to all sense of obligation, who stigmatize with your contempt the playthings of your passions – your unfortunate victims! It's you who ought to be punished for the errors of our youth – you and your magistrates so vain of their right to judge us, you who by your culpable negligence allow us to be deprived of all honest means of existence. What is there for these unhappy girls to do? They had a natural right to make all feminine apparel and yet they let thousands of men be trained to it.

[**Figaro** (*furiously*)   They even set soldiers to embroidery!]

Marceline (*carried away by her own eloquence*)   Even in the more exalted walks of life you accord us women no more than a derisory consideration. In a state of servitude behind the alluring pretences of respect, treated as children where our possessions are concerned we are punished as responsible adults where our faults are in question! Ah! Whatever way one looks at it your conduct towards us must provoke horror or compassion!

[**Figaro**   She's right!
The Count (*aside*)   All too much so.
Brid'oison   My God! How right she is!]

Marceline   But what if an unjust man denies us justice, my son? Think no more about whence you came but whither you are bound. That is all that matters to any of us. Within a few months your fiancée will be her own mistress: she'll accept you: that I'll answer for. Live, then, henceforward in company of a loving wife and mother who will be rivals only in affection for you. Be indulgent towards them and rejoice in your happiness, my son; be gay, free, open-hearted with all the world: your mother will seek no other happiness.

Lucretia from *Lucretia Borgia* by Victor Hugo (translated by Richard Hand)

Lucretia Borgia is a melodramatic prose tragedy based on the legend of the Borgias. It is set in sixteenth-century Italy and was first performed in Paris in 1833.

The infamous Borgias are a byword for butchery, sexual perversity and machiavellian politics. Born into a family where treachery, adultery, murder, incest and betrayal were the norm, Lucretia has emerged a depraved and pitiless woman. Her only saving grace is her love for her son, Gennaro, to whom she gave birth in secret and hid to protect him from her villainous relatives.

At the beginning of the play Lucretia comes to Venice in disguise to be reunited with Gennaro, now a handsome twenty-year-old Venetian soldier who is blissfully unaware of his parentage. Gennaro's life is driven by his love for the mother he has never seen, and his desire to be worthy of her. When Lucretia declares her love for him, Gennaro feels a deep attraction for this beautiful and sympathetic woman, unaware of her identity. When his friends learn of this 'romantic' encounter they name her in front of Gennaro as the notorious Lucretia Borgia, a woman who evokes fear and horror across Italy. Gennaro is repelled and Lucretia vows to take revenge on his friends for betraying her and alienating Gennaro. They have made a dangerous enemy.

In this scene Gennaro and friends have come to Ferrara as part of a Venetian delegation. They have been invited to dine at the palace of the Princess Negroni, which adjoins Lucretia's palace. They drink and carouse, but revelry turns to horror as a line of heavily cowled monks enter the dining hall singing an ominous plainsong for the dead. Realising they have been lured into a trap, the friends draw their swords just as a regal and triumphant Lucretia sweeps in to tell them the wine they have been drinking is poisoned – they will be dead within the hour! As the horrified soldiers realise what she has done, Lucretia relishes the sweetness of her revenge, goading them with past crimes committed against their families, mercilessly revealing five coffins already prepared for their imminent demise.

But her triumph turns to despair when she discovers that her beloved son is among their company. Gennaro, however, has an antidote and will wreak his revenge.

———————

Lucretia Just a few days ago, every one of you gloated over my name in triumph. Now you utter my name in terror. Yes, look at me with those eyes filled with dread. It really is Lucretia Borgia, my fine gentlemen. I have some important news to tell you. You are all dying, gentlemen. You have all been poisoned and will be dead within the hour. Do not attempt to escape. The adjoining room is full of guards. Now, it is my turn. My turn to bellow out your names and crush you in the palm of my hand. Jeppo Liveretto, time to join your uncle Vitelli, who was stabbed to death in the Vatican cellars on my orders! Ascanio Petrucci, time to join your cousin Pandolfo whom I murdered to steal his city! Oloferno Vitellozzo, your uncle Iago d'Appiani awaits you; he, too, was poisoned at a banquet! Maffio Orsini, you can talk about me in the afterlife with your brother Gravina whom I strangled in his sleep! Apostolo Gazella, I had your father Francisco Gazella beheaded, I slit the throat of your cousin Alfonso d'Aragon, it is time for you to join them! Upon my soul, I was your guest at a ball in Venice, I return the compliment with a banquet in Ferrara! A feast for a feast, gentlemen!

[**Jeppo** Maffio, tell me it's a nightmare!
Maffio God help us!]

Lucretia Ah! My young friends from Venice! Did you really not expect this? My God! I think I am sufficiently avenged! What do you think, gentlemen? Who knows the meaning of the word 'revenge' here? You have all tasted it tonight! Tell me what you think? I'd call it a triumph of revenge – all planned and executed by a mere woman too! (*To the* **Monks**.) My fathers, take these men into the adjoining chamber, take their confession, and in the few moments that remain to them in this mortal life you may try and save what is left of their souls! Gentlemen, if any of you have souls feel free to confess – you are in good hands. These holy fathers are monks at Saint Sixtus, and have on occasions like this been given dispensation from the Pope himself to assist me! Yes, I have taken care of your souls just as I will take care of your bodies. Behold! Clear a space, fathers, so that these gentlemen may see. (*The* **Monks** *in front of the doorway move away and in so doing reveal five coffins*

draped in black cloth.) Five coffins, gentlemen. One for each of you!
Ah, you young fools! Did you think you could rip out the guts of a
wretched woman and expect no retribution! Look, Jeppo and
Maffio, there are your coffins! Oloferno, Apostolo, Ascanio, there are
yours! Five coffins for the five of you!

Mathilde from *Caprice* by Alfred de Musset (translated by Donald Watson)

Caprice is a beautifully crafted one-act play with an elegant proverb about fidelity and married love at its heart. Written in 1837, it was Musset's first success.

Monsieur de Chavigny has been married to Mathilde for a year. Although he loves her, he is beginning to seek his pleasures elsewhere. While he is out 'on the town', Mathilde makes him a little red purse to demonstrate how often he is in her thoughts, and to gently remind him of his neglect. She is just about to give it to him when he produces another one – a present, it seems from a rival. Mathilde begs him, on her knees, to give it to her in exchange for her own love token, but Chavigny refuses and leaves for a ball, angry that she should have humiliated herself.

Mathilde is an innocent, loving twenty-year-old – a good little wife who is described by her more sophisticated friend, Madame de Lery, to be 'as lovely as a rose and faithful as a spaniel'. She adores her husband and is heartbroken by his rejection and the thought that he has fallen for someone else. The difficulty with this speech is how to avoid making it sound sentimental or mawkish, and how to make sense of a young woman talking to her purse! Remember that Mathilde is left on her own a great deal. The little purse has taken her two weeks to make. It has given her something to do during her husband's frequent absences. Like a lonely child talking to a soft toy, it seems her only friend. There is nobody else to share her feelings with so the rejected purse becomes a symbol of her love and the way she feels her husband treats her. She is jealous, miserable and about to throw the purse in the fire – but it feels like throwing her love away, so she puts it next to her heart in the hope that her husband might come back and find it.

By the end of the play, the clever Madame de Lery has taught Chavigny the lesson that friendship and a constant wife are worth more than any caprice and, via her agency, the couple are reunited.

Mathilde   Well, if it cannot be that one, this is the one I shall burn. (*She goes to her desk and takes out the purse she has made.*) Poor little purse! Just now I touched you with my lips. Remember what I whispered? We were too late, you see. He does not want you. And now he does not want me either. (*She moves to the fireplace.*) How foolish we are to live on dreams. They never come true. What is that fatal charm which makes us cherish our illusions? Why does it give such pleasure to nurse an idle fancy, and then in secret try and bring it to fruition? What good does it do? It only leads to tears. Fate is too capricious. What more does it want of us? How many prayers, how much cautious preparation, before it fulfils the meanest of our hopes? You were right, Monsieur le Comte, to say I was childish to be so insistent. But how I enjoyed insisting! And what of you? Proud or inconstant as you are, it would have cost so little to pander to my childish whim. Oh no! He no longer loves me, loves me no more. It is you he loves, Madame de Blainville! (*She weeps.*) Now . . . not another thought! I will throw this . . . plaything into the fire. It was not ready in time. Yet even if he had received it tonight, he would surely have lost it tomorrow! Yes, of course he would! He would have left my purse lying around on some table, among his old junk, Heaven knows where, while that other purse would never leave his side! I can see him now, at his gambling, proudly take it from his pocket and cast it down on the green baize, with the gold coins jingling inside. And now I *am* jealous: what more does an unhappy wife need to make her husband hate her! (*She is about to throw the purse on the fire, then she stops.*) But what have you done? Why destroy you? I made you with my own hands, an unlucky token of my love. It is no fault of yours. You were waiting and hoping too. That cruel scene between us did not turn you pale. Your colour is bright as ever. I feel quite fond of you. Two whole weeks of my life are caught up in your fine threads. No! Oh no! These hands that made you will not murder you. I want to save you and complete my work on you. Like a relic close to my heart you will make me happy and sad. Reminding me of my love for him, of his neglect and his caprices. And who knows but he might come back again, to seek you out in your secret hiding-place?

Agafya from *Marriage* by Nikolai Gogol (translated by Stephen Mulrine)

This unsentimental comic masterpiece, appropriately sub-titled 'a thoroughly improbable event in two acts', premiered in St Petersburg in 1842.

It tells the story of a plump, pretty, rich girl, Agafya, whose family decides it is time for her to marry. A devious old matchmaker, Fyokla Ivanova, is dispatched to find her a husband but she comes up with a bevy of highly unsuitable candidates with hilarious consequences.

At this point, Agafya has been introduced to the suitors and is alone, considering her options. There's Anuchkin, a retired infantry officer who's a bit of a rough diamond but nevertheless insists his wife speaks French. Mr Podkolyosin, a stout, stammering civil servant – and a confirmed bachelor, who has been press-ganged into marrying by his friend. Omelet, an elderly and irascible office manager, more interested in her money than herself, and Zhevakin (Baltazar), a handsome but penurious naval officer 'who likes them on the plump side'. What a choice! If only she could meld all their good points together into one man.

Agafya is no more motivated by love than her self-interested suitors. She is a shallow, snobbish, graceless creature whose main agenda is social advancement. She is probably a little too long in the tooth to be looking for a husband, and getting a bit desperate. But that doesn't stop her being choosy. She is on tenterhooks of anxiety and becomes increasingly agitated as she wrestles with her choices, trying to pick the best of a bad bunch. What if she makes a mistake? How better to choose than put all their names into the 'hat' to see which one prevails? Let fate decide. (Don't get hung up on the props – the text is so graphic, the play could have been written for radio. A simple mime with your handbag will suffice.)

It is well documented that Gogol wasn't a great fan of marriage or the family. There is no happy ending. Agafya is railroaded into choosing Podkolyosin, but he turns out to be a commitmentphobe, who jumps out of the window and escapes just in the nick of time!

Agafya (*alone*) Honestly, this choosing business is so difficult. If there were just one or two, but four! Take your pick. Mr Anuchkin isn't bad-looking, but he's a bit skinny, of course. And Mr Podkolyosin isn't too bad, either. And truth to tell, though he's rather stout, Mr Omelet's still a fine figure of a man. So what am I to do, if you please? Mr Zhevakin's also a man of distinction. It really is difficult to decide, you can't begin to describe it. Now, if you could attach Mr Anuchkin's lips to Mr Podkolyosin's nose, and take some of Mr Zhevakin's easy manner, and perhaps add Mr Omelet's solid build, I could decide on the spot. But now I've got to rack my brains! And it's giving me a fearsome headache. I think it'd be best to draw lots. Turn the whole matter over to God's will, and whichever one comes out, that'll be my husband. I'll write all their names on bits of paper, roll them up tight, then so be it. (*She goes over to her desk, takes out scissors and paper, cuts it up into slips, writes on them, and rolls them up, still talking.*) Life's so trying for a girl, especially when she's in love. It's something no man will ever understand, and anyway they just don't want to. Now, that's them ready! All that remains is to put them in my purse, shut my eyes, and that's it – what will be, will be. (*Puts the slips of paper into her purse and gives it a shake.*) This is dreadful . . . oh God, please make it Mr Anuchkin! No, why him? Better Mr Podkolyosin. But why Mr Podkolyosin? In what way are the others worse? No, no, I won't . . . whichever comes out, so be it. (*She rummages in her purse and pulls them all out instead of one.*) Oh! All of them! They've all come out! And my heart's pounding. No, no, it's got to be one! (*Puts the slips back in her purse and mixes them. At that moment* **Kochkaryov** *stealthily enters and stands behind her.*) Oh, if only I could draw out Baltazar . . . no, what am I saying? I mean Mr Anuchkin . . . no, I won't, I won't. Let fate decide.

Darya Ivanovna from *A Provincial Lady* by Ivan Turgenev (translated by David Garnett)

This is a delicate one-act comedy written in 1851. It is set in an unnamed provincial town in the home of Alexey Stupendyev, a middle-aged, unprepossessing district clerk.

Darya Ivanovna is his wife. At twenty-eight, she is twenty years his junior. She feels she is a cut above her husband and is vegetating as a wife to a down-at-heel government official. She has been eagerly awaiting a visit from Count Lyubin who is high up in the government service in St Petersburg. The Count's mother was Darya's benefactress, and although of lowly birth, she was brought up on her grand estate where she met the Count twelve years ago. He had amused himself by flirting with his mother's pretty protégée and she had harboured unrealistic dreams of romance. She has staked a lot on this visit, hoping the Count will remember her so she can use the connection to get a better job for her husband in St Petersburg. She longs for the high life of the city. Society. Fashion. Excitement. But when the Count arrives, he scarcely recognises her. Nor is he as she remembers him. He has become a middle-aged dandy, wrinkled and powdered with dyed hair. What a disappointment! Nevertheless, he is her ticket out of this dreary provincial life and she is determined to use him to escape.

Thinking aloud, she mulls over the position. The prospect of achieving her ends has started to look slim. Perhaps all he sees is a downtrodden provincial wife? But the more she thinks about it, the more her resolve hardens. Half her life is over. She isn't asking a great deal after all. This might be her last chance to change her fortunes. If she can't, then she deserves everything she gets. Her excitement mounts as she embraces the challenge. The speech begins on a despondent note but soon gathers momentum as a battle plan begins to take shape. The prospect of changing her life is exciting and frightening at the same time and if it involves charming, flattering and flirting with this less than appetising fellow – so be it.

By the time the Count returns, she is decorously lounging on the sofa with a book, thoroughly psyched up for the fray.

Darya (*remains for some time motionless*)   He didn't take the slightest notice of me – that's clear. He has forgotten me. And it seems I was foolish to have expected anything from his coming. What hopes I've been building on his visit . . . (*Looks round her.*) Am I to remain here for ever, here? Well, there's no help for it! (*A pause.*) It's not quite certain yet, though. He has scarcely seen me. . . . (*Glancing in the looking-glass.*) I don't dye my hair, at any rate . . . We'll see, we'll see. (*Walks up and down the room, goes to the piano and plays a few chords.*) This suspense is a torture. (*Sits down on sofa.*) But perhaps I too have run to seed in this wretched little town . . . How can I tell? Who is there here to say what I'm like now, who is there who can make me feel what I've become? I'm superior to all of them, unhappily . . . I'm above their level; but in his eyes – I'm none the less a provincial, the wife of a local clerk, his mother's old protégée, married off somehow . . . while he, he is a distinguished man, high up in the service, wealthy . . . well, he's not exactly wealthy; his affairs are in a bad way in Petersburg, and I expect he'll be here for a good deal more than a month. He's good-looking, that is he was good-looking . . . now he powders and dyes his hair. They say that to men of his age the memories of young days are particularly precious; he knew me twelve years ago, he flirted with me . . . Yes, yes, of course he had nothing better to do, that's why he flirted with me, but still . . . (*Sighs.*) And in those days I remember I dreamed . . . the dreams one has at sixteen! (*Suddenly draws herself up erect.*) Good heavens, I do believe I have still one of his letters . . . I'm sure I have. But where is it? How annoying that I didn't think of it before! . . . I've still time, though . . . (*A pause.*) Well, we shall see. And how lucky the music and books came just now! It makes me laugh . . . Like a general before a battle, I'm preparing to meet the enemy . . . And how I have changed in these last years! Can this be me, so coolly, so calmly thinking over what I'm to do? Necessity will drive one to learn anything, and to unlearn many things. No, I'm not calm, I'm excited now, but only because I don't know whether I can succeed . . . Come, is that so? I'm not a girl now, of course, and memories have become precious to me, too . . . such as they are . . . I shall have no others, and half my life, more than half

100

is over. (*Smiles.*) But they are a long time. And what do I ask? What am I struggling for? The merest nothing. For him to give us a chance to move to Petersburg, to find us a post there – is nothing. And Alexey Ivanitch will be glad of any post . . . Can I fail to get even that? If so, it's right I should stay in a provincial town . . . I deserve nothing better . . . (*Pressing her hands to her cheeks.*) I'm in a fever with this suspense, these thoughts; my cheeks are simply burning. (*A pause.*) Well, so much the better. (*Hearing a sound in the study.*) They are coming . . . the battle is beginning . . . Oh cowardly, ill-timed fears, away with you! (*Takes up a book and leans back on the sofa.* **Stupendyev** *and* **Count Lyubin** *come in.*)

Katerina from *The Thunderstorm* by Alexander Ostrovsky (translated by Andrew MacAndrew)

This was first performed in 1859 and hailed as Ostrovsky's masterpiece. It is set in a Kalinov, a small hidebound country town on the banks of the River Volga. Ostrovsky was writing about the narrow-minded greed of nineteenth-century 'Old Russia' – a society exemplified by the self-serving, autocratic merchant class who ruled the roost like petty tyrants. It is a poignant human tragedy about the clash between romantic idealism and harsh reality.

Katerina is a free spirit, an ardent, sensitive young woman who finds her dreamy, spiritual nature crushed by an unhappy marriage, the rigid atmosphere of her husband's merchant family and the domestic tyranny of her mother-in-law. Yearning for love and happiness she falls in love with Boris, the handsome Moscow-educated nephew of another wealthy merchant, who seems so different from everybody else. Her one ally is her rebellious sister-in-law, Barbara, with whom she shares her feelings of love and desperation. When Katerina's spineless husband goes on a trip, Barbara finds the key to the back gate and gives it to Katerina, offering to tell Boris to meet her there. With the key burning in her hand, Katerina is consumed by a fever of excitement and apprehension. Torn between religious stricture and longed-for escape, she wrestles with temptation. To leave the house to meet another man would be the most unthinkable breach of civilised behaviour, yet every bone in her body aches for Boris. All her thoughts focus on the key – the symbol of her freedom – as she holds it, rejects it, contemplates it, hides it – arguing with herself over the dangers and opportunities it offers, until finally convincing herself to 'seize the day' before all hope of happiness is lost.

The play has the remorseless progress of Greek tragedy, ending with Katerina jumping into the Volga during the thunderstorm of the title – her suicide an act of repentance for her adultery and escape from an impossible situation.

Katerina (*holding key in hand*)   What's she doing? The things she thinks up! Ah, she's mad, mad! It would be the end of me! I must throw the key away, into the river, so that no one'll ever find it! It's burning my hand like a hot coal. (*Thinks a while.*) Yes, that's the way a woman gets lost! Who can be happy being shut up like me? All kinds of things keep cropping up in a woman's head, when she's locked up like this. And so, when she gets the chance, she throws herself at it. But how can one do anything without thinking it over, weighing what'll come of it? It doesn't take long to get into trouble and after that you'll regret it all your life and your bondage will be even more bitter than before. (*Pause.*) Ah, but it's a bitter bondage. It's bad enough as it is! People cry over being locked in, especially us women. Take me, I'm bored, I'm tormented by all sorts of things and I don't see any way out! It'll only get worse and worse with time. And now, that sinful thing . . . (*Sinks into thought.*) Ah, if it wasn't for my mother-in-law! She's made me hate this house. By now I loathe the very walls. (*Looks dreamily at the key.*) Shall I throw it away? Of course I must! Why am I holding it in my hand in the first place? It was given to tempt me, to bring about my perdition. (*Listens.*) Ah, someone's coming. Oh, that scared me! (*Hides the key in her pocket.*) No, no one's coming. Why did I have to get so frightened? Why did I hide the key? . . . Well, all right, let it stay in my pocket. I suppose my fate is written that way in the book. And anyway, what's wrong if I only glance at him from a distance? Even if I talked to him the way other people talk to each other, what'd be so bad about that? But what about the promise I made to Tikhon? But then, he didn't even want me to make that oath! And possibly I'll never get another opportunity like this in my life. Then I'll never forgive myself for having let it slip by. Well, what's the point of lying to myself? Even if I had to die, I would still see him if I could. For whose benefit am I putting all this on? Throw away the key? Not on your life! It's mine now. Whatever happens, I will see Boris! Ah, I wish it were night!

Natalia from *A Month in the Country* by Ivan Turgenev (translated by Andrew MacAndrew)

Written during the 1840s, *A Month in the Country* was banned by the censor and in consequence was not staged until 1872. It is a tragicomedy about bourgeois Russian life in the early 1840s set on a country estate near Moscow.

Natalia is the twenty-nine-year-old wife of rich, hard-working landowner, Arkady Islaev, and guardian to Vera, a seventeen-year-old orphan. Natalia has recently appointed a handsome student, Alexei Balaev, as tutor for her young son and both she and Vera have fallen in love with him.

A lonely, intelligent, sensual woman past the first flush of youth, Natalia is practised at charming others to get what she wants. Life on the estate is tedious, broken only by visits from the local doctor and an old family friend, Michel Rakitin, who is in love with her. Her husband is kindly but has no concept of his wife's nature or needs. Balaev's youth and vigour make her feel alive again.

Here Natalia, in a 'motherly' chat, suggests to Vera that she consider marrying their stodgy, middle-aged, well-off neighbour, Bolshintsov, to secure her future. Vera thinks she is joking and rejects the idea. Natalia fishes for a reason why Vera may not be keen to marry and by manipulative questioning wheedles her feelings for Balaev out of her.

Discovering she has a much younger rival for Balaev's affections shakes Natalia to the core, and forces her to face up to her feelings. She bombards herself with uncomfortable questions. (Look at the graphic stage directions. These give an insight into her bewildered and restless state of mind.) Should she pursue Balaev, marry Vera off to Bolshintsov, succumb to Rakitin or settle for her 'good and trusting' husband? In an unchecked stream of consciousness, a jumble of self-denigration, desperation, frustration, jealousy, misery and self-doubt, she flits from thought to thought expressed in half-finished sentences and shifting moods, but overarching all is this new passionate feeling which consumes her like a lovelorn teenager and knocks her off her feet.

Natalia (*remaining alone and motionless for a short while*) Now I see it
all. Those two children love each other. (*Stops and passes a hand across
her face.*) Well, why not? So much the better. I hope they'll be very
happy! (*Laughing.*) Ah, how could I have even thought . . . (*Stops
again.*) It didn't take her long to let the cat out of the bag. I admit I
never suspected . . . in fact, the news has quite shaken me. But wait a
while, it's not over yet. Oh, my God, what am I saying? What's the
matter with me? I don't recognize myself. Have I come to that?
(*Pause.*) What am I doing? I want to give that poor girl away in
marriage to an old man. I'm trying to use the doctor . . . he suspects,
makes hints . . . Then there's Arkady, and Rakitin. Ah . . . (*She
shudders and suddenly throws back her head.*) But, it's really too much.
Me jealous of Vera? Can I be . . . can I really have fallen in love with
him? (*Pause.*) What, do you still doubt it? Yes, you're in love, you
wretched woman! How it happened, I don't know. It's as if I'd been
poisoned. Suddenly everything's shattered and confused. He's afraid
of me. Everyone's afraid of me. And what could he possibly see in
me? What would he want with someone like me? He's young and
she's young. And I! (*Bitterly.*) Ah, how could he understand me?
They're both silly just as Rakitin says. Ah, that one, I can't stand him
for being so clever! And Arkady, my good, trusting Arkady! Oh God, I
wish I were dead! (*Rising.*) But, good heavens, I must be going out of
my mind! Why exaggerate, after all? Well, all right, I've received a
blow. I'm not accustomed . . . it's the first time I . . . yes, the first
time! It's the first time I've ever been in love! (*Sitting down again.*) He
must leave. Yes. And Rakitin, too. It's time I took hold of myself. I
allowed myself to step out of line – and now look how far I've gone.
And what is it I like about him? (*Growing thoughtful.*) So that's what it
is, this frightening feeling. Oh Arkady! I'll fling myself into his arms
and beg him to forgive me, to protect me, to save me – him and no
one else! All the rest are outsiders to me and they must remain
outsiders. But is there really . . . can there really be no other way out?
This girl – she's just a child. She could be mistaken. It's all a lot of
childish nonsense. Why am I . . . I'll have the matter out with him,
I'll ask him . . . (*Reproachfully.*) What's this? You still have hopes? You
still want to hope? And what am I hoping for! Oh God, oh God,
don't let me despise myself! (*She buries her face in her hands.*)

Mrs Alving from *Ghosts* by Henrik Ibsen (translated by Michael Meyer)

Written in 1881, *Ghosts* is a domestic tragedy set on Mrs Alving's country estate on a fjord in western Norway. Many theatres rejected it in its day because of its subject matter, which deals with venereal disease and incest. It received its first performance in Chicago in 1883.

Mrs Alving, the middle-aged widow of Captain Alving, a much respected chamberlain to the king, is making preparations for the opening of an orphanage in memory of her husband. To her delight, Oswald, their ailing artist son, has made a rare visit from Paris for the celebrations to honour his father.

In this scene Pastor Manders is visiting to discuss business matters relating to the orphanage, and has just had a disturbing conversation with Oswald about free love, open marriage and the bohemian life of a Parisian artist – views with which Mrs Alving expresses sympathy. The Pastor is horrified and blames Mrs Alving for her son's loose attitudes, reminding her of past sins – how, when young, she left her husband, abandoned her child and he persuaded her to return by reminding her of her reputation and wifely duties. His moralising, judgemental attitude stings Mrs Alving into telling him the truth about her marriage and the reasons for sending Oswald away.

She tells Manders how she sustained her husband's public reputation and endured his dissolute behaviour until his death from syphilis. How, when he got her housekeeper pregnant, it was the last straw, and how, to protect her young son from moral contamination, she sent him away.

Mrs Alving is an intelligent, industrious woman of great strength and forbearance. She has sustained an illusion of respectability throughout her married life, but paid a high price for it. Unable to leave a miserable marriage in the face of pressure from Manders and society's narrow expectations, her selfless love for Oswald has enabled her to bear the most painful separation rather than see him come to harm. The welfare of her son is paramount. Even now, the memorial she has built to her husband's memory is designed to perpetuate the myth of his unblemished reputation and protect Oswald from the truth. But Mrs Alving is beginning to understand that she must seek a different road to happiness and freedom from the strictures that have dogged her life.

Mrs Alving But now, Manders, now I shall tell the truth. I have sworn to myself that one day you should know it. Only you.

[**Manders** And what is the truth?].

Mrs Alving The truth is that my husband died just as dissolute as he had always lived.

[**Manders** (*gropes for a chair*) What did you say?]

Mrs Alving Just as dissolute, at any rate in his desires, after nineteen years of marriage, as he was before you wedded us.

[**Manders** You call these youthful escapades – these irregularities – excesses, if you like – evidence of a dissolute life!

Mrs Alving That is the expression our doctor used.

Manders I don't understand you.

Mrs Alving It doesn't matter.

Manders I cannot believe my ears. You mean your whole married life – all those years you shared with your husband – were nothing but a façade!

Mrs Alving Yes. Now you know.

Manders But – but this I cannot accept! I don't understand – I cannot credit it! But how on earth is it possible – how could such a thing be kept secret?]

Mrs Alving I had to fight, day after day, to keep it secret. After Oswald was born I thought things became a little better with Alving. But it didn't last long. And now I had to fight a double battle, fight with all my strength to prevent anyone knowing what kind of a man my child's father was. And you know what a winning personality Alving had. No one could believe anything but good of him. He was one of those people whose reputations remained untarnished by the way they live. But then, Manders – you must know this too – then came the most loathsome thing of all.

[**Manders** More loathsome than this!]

Mrs Alving I had put up with him, although I knew well what went on secretly outside the house. But when he offended within our four walls –

[**Manders** What are you saying? Here!]

Mrs Alving Yes, here in our own home. In there – (*Points to the*

108

first door on the right.) – it was in the dining-room I first found out about it. I had something to do in there and the door was standing ajar. Then I heard our maid come up from the garden to water the flowers in there.

[**Manders** Oh, yes?]

Mrs Alving A few moments later I heard Alving enter the room. He said something to her. And then I heard – (*Gives a short laugh.*) – I still don't know whether to laugh or cry – I heard my own servant whisper: 'Stop it, Mr Alving! Let me go!'

[**Manders** What an unseemly frivolity! But it was nothing more than a frivolity, Mrs Alving. Believe me.]

Mrs Alving I soon found out what to believe. My husband had his way with the girl. And that relationship had consequences, Pastor Manders.

[**Manders** (*petrified*) And all this took place in this house! In this house!]

Mrs Alving I had endured much in this house. To keep him at home in the evenings – and at night – I had to make myself his companion in his secret dissipations up in his room. There I had to sit alone with him, had to clink my glass with his and drink with him, listen to his obscene and senseless drivelling, had to fight him with my fists to haul him into bed –

[**Manders** (*shocked*) I don't know how you managed to endure it.
Mrs Alving *I had to, for my little son's sake.*]

But when the final humiliation came – when my own servant – then I swore to myself: 'This must stop!' And so I took over the reins of this house; both as regards him and everything else. For now, you see, I had a weapon against him; he dared not murmur. It was then that I sent Oswald away. He was nearly seven and was beginning to notice things and ask questions, the way children do. I couldn't bear that, Manders. I thought the child could not help but be poisoned merely by breathing in this tainted home. That was why I sent him away. And so now you know why he was never allowed to set foot in his home while his father was alive. No one knows what it cost me.

109

Yelena from *Uncle Vanya* by Anton Chekhov (translated by Michael Frayn)

Chekhov is considered the father of modern drama. His reputation as a dramatist rests on four masterpieces written in the last ten years of his life. This one, *Uncle Vanya*, was first performed at the Moscow Art Theatre in 1898.

Uncle Vanya is a tragicomedy set on a remote country estate where Sonya and her Uncle Vanya have laboured for years to support Sonya's father, the selfish, gout-ridden Professor Serebriakov and his spirited young second wife, Yelena, in St Petersburg. When the couple come to visit, daily routines are disrupted and passions flare as the characters struggle with their disappointments, regrets and frustrated loves.

Sonya has just confided in her stepmother about her love for Astrov, the local doctor, who is a frequent visitor to the estate. Yelena suspects that he has another motive for coming, but nevertheless promises to discover discreetly whether Astrov returns Sonya's feelings. The plain girl leaves in a state of great agitation and Yelena is left alone to reflect aloud on the confidence Sonya has shared.

Yelena is a beautiful, purposeless, bored, languorous, self-absorbed, provocative woman in her thirties. All the men are attracted to her. Her marriage to the pompous old professor has become tiresome. She is desperately unhappy and feels she has wasted her youth in a sterile marriage. She is not a 'country person' and can find nothing entertaining on the estate. When Astrov visits he brings vitality and interesting ideas. He is a free spirit and brightens their world. She can't help smiling when she thinks of him. Although she has little real empathy with Sonya's plight (empathy is not in her nature) she understands completely why she finds Astrov attractive. We see how very taken with him she is herself. She is more of a rival than a confidante and her guilt is more self-dramatising than genuine.

Although Vanya sees Yelena as a wild, independent woman she knows she is too weak and cowardly to do anything but endure the life she has chosen.

Yelena (*alone*) Is there anything worse than knowing the secrets of another's heart and not being able to help? (*Reflects.*) He's not in love with her, that's plain enough, but why shouldn't he marry her? She's not beautiful, but for a country doctor, at his age, she'd make a fine wife. She's intelligent, she's kind and good . . . That's all beside the point, though, that's all beside the point . . . (*Pause.*) I know how it is for that poor child. In the midst of all this desperate boredom, where all the people around her are just perambulating grey blobs, where every word spoken is vile, where there's nothing going on but eating, drinking, and sleeping, *he* makes one of his occasional appearances; and he's not like the others – he's handsome, he's interesting, he's fascinating – and it's like the bright moon rising in the midst of darkness . . . To fall under the spell of a man like that, to forget oneself . . . I think I've become slightly fascinated, too. When he's not here, yes, I'm bored – and now here I am smiling at the thought of him . . . Uncle Vanya tells me I have mermaid's blood in my veins. 'Run wild for once in your life . . .' So – perhaps that's what I should do . . . Fly off as free as a bird away from all of you, away from your half-asleep faces, away from all this talk – forget your very existence . . . But I'm a coward, I'm too timid . . . I should be tormented by conscience . . . I feel guilty as it is, with his coming here every day – because I can guess why he comes – I'm already almost down on my knees in front of Sonya, weeping and begging her to forgive me . . .

Irena Serghyeevna from *Three Sisters* by Anton Chekhov (translated by Elisaveta Fen)

Three Sisters premiered at the Moscow Art Theatre in 1901. It is set in the Prozorovs' house in a country town about a thousand miles from Moscow. The longing for happiness, unrequited love, the dissolution of dreams and the casual damage time inflicts are among the themes it addresses.

The Prozorov sisters' recently deceased father brought them from Moscow more than a decade ago. They are well-educated young women who dream of escape from their purposeless provincial lives to a Moscow they have romanticised since childhood – a place where they will find happiness and a solution to their problems.

Their spineless brother, Andrey, has married a manipulative and ambitious local woman, scuppering the family's hopes of social advancement. His soul-destroying marriage and a couple of young children have sapped his will and driven him to gambling.

In Act 3 there is a fire in the locality. Everyone has rallied round to help, but Andrey just stays in his room, playing the violin. A disgusted Masha has just told Irena that Andrey has mortgaged the family home to the bank, without consultation, to fend off his creditors.

Irena, the youngest sister, believed work would save her from an aimless existence, but has been disappointed. The optimistic high spirits of her twentieth birthday party three years earlier, her hopes of finding love and returning to her beloved Moscow have been eroded by the daily grind of a job in the telegraph office. Andrey has let them down, her tyrannical sister-in-law schemes to oust them from their father's house, and out of desperation she is contemplating a loveless marriage to the unprepossessing Baron Toozenbach. The thought of Andrey's duplicity and inertia serves to underline everything that is wrong with her life and triggers a storm of self-pity and frustrated sobs. She feels her intellect is being subsumed and her youth and hopes are disappearing. It all seems too much to bear.

Irena   The truth is that Andrey is getting to be shallow-minded. He's ageing and since he's been living with that woman he's lost all the inspiration he used to have! Not long ago he was working for a professorship, and yet yesterday he boasted of having at last been elected a member of the County Council. Fancy him a member, with Protopopov as chairman! They say the whole town's laughing at him, he's the only one who doesn't know anything or see anything. And now, you see, everyone's at the fire, while he's just sitting in his room, not taking the slightest notice of it. Just playing his violin. (*Agitated.*) Oh, how dreadful it is, how dreadful, how dreadful! I can't bear it any longer, I can't, I really can't! . . .

[*Enter* **Olga**. *She starts arranging things on her bedside table.*]

(*Sobs loudly.*) You must turn me out of here! Turn me out; I can't stand it any more!

[**Olga** (*alarmed*)   What is it? What is it, darling?]

Irena (*sobbing*)   Where . . . Where has it all gone to? Where is it? Oh, God! I've forgotten . . . I've forgotten everything . . . there's nothing but a muddle in my head . . . I don't remember what the Italian for 'window' is, or for 'ceiling' . . . Every day I'm forgetting more and more, and life's slipping by, and it will never, never come back . . . We shall never go to Moscow . . . I can see that we shall never go . . .

[**Olga**   Don't, my dear, don't . . .]

Irena (*trying to control herself*)   Oh, I'm so miserable! . . . I can't work, I won't work! I've had enough of it, enough! . . . First I worked on the telegraph, now I'm in the County Council office, and I hate and despise everything they give me to do there . . . I'm twenty-three years old, I've been working all this time, and I feel as if my brain's dried up. I know I've got thinner and uglier and older, and I find no kind of satisfaction in anything, none at all. And the time's passing . . . and I feel as if I'm moving away from any hope of a genuine, fine life, I'm moving further and further away and sinking into a kind of abyss. I feel in despair, and I don't know why I'm still alive, why I haven't killed myself . . .

Acknowledgements

p. 9   extract from *Persians* by Aeschylus (translated by Kenneth McLeish and Frederic Raphael), Methuen Publishing Ltd. Translation copyright © 1991 by the Estate of Kenneth McLeish. Performance rights: Alan Brodie Representation Ltd, London (info@alanbrodie.com)

p. 88   extract from *The Barber of Seville & The Marriage of Figaro* by Beaumarchais (translated and with an introduction by John Wood), Penguin Books, 1964. Translation copyright © 1964 by John Wood. Performance rights: please apply in the first instance to Penguin Group UK, London (adultpermissions @penguin.co.uk)

p. 67   extract from *The Surgeon of Honour* by Calderón de la Barca (translated by Gwynne Edwards), Methuen Publishing Ltd. Translation copyright © 1991 by Gwynne Edwards. Performance rights (amateur): Samuel French Ltd, London (theatre@samuel french-london.co.uk)

p. 113   extract from *Three Sisters* (taken from *Plays*) by Anton Chekhov (translated with an introduction by Elisaveta Fen), Penguin Classics, 1951, (reprinted 1954). Translation copyright © 1951, 1954 by Elisaveta Fen. Performance rights: please apply in the first instance to Penguin Group UK, London (adultpermissions @penguin.co.uk)

p. 111   extract from *Uncle Vanya* by Anton Chekhov (translated by Michael Frayn), Methuen Publishing Ltd. Translation copyright © 1988, 1991 by Michael Frayn. Performance rights (professional): PFD, London (gsmart@pfd.co.uk). Performance rights (amateur): Samuel French Ltd (theatre@samuelfrench-london.co.uk)

p. 95   extract from *Caprice* by Alfred de Musset (translated by Donald Watson), Methuen Publishing Ltd. Translation copyright © 1995 by Donald Watson. Performance rights: Methuen Publishing Ltd (rights@methuen.co.uk)

116

Disclaimer